JUST US

ALSO BY CLAUDIA RANKINE

Poetry

Citizen: An American Lyric
Don't Let Me Be Lonely: An American Lyric
Plot
The End of the Alphabet
Nothing in Nature Is Private

Plays

Help
The White Card
The Provenance of Beauty: A South Bronx Travelogue

Coeditor

The Racial Imaginary
American Poets in the 21st Century
American Women Poets in the 21st Century

JUST US

AN AMERICAN CONVERSATION

CLAUDIA RANKINE

Graywolf Press

Permission acknowledgments appear on pp. 337–339.

This publication is made possible, in part, by the voters of Minnesota through a Minnesota State Arts Board Operating Support grant, thanks to a legislative appropriation from the arts and cultural heritage fund. Significant support has also been provided by Target Foundation, the McKnight Foundation, the Lannan Foundation, the Amazon Literary Partnership, and other generous contributions from foundations, corporations, and individuals. To these organizations and individuals we offer our heartfelt thanks.

Published by Graywolf Press
250 Third Avenue North, Suite 600
Minneapolis, Minnesota 55401

www.graywolfpress.org

Published in the United States of America

ISBN 978-1-64445-021-5 (cloth)
ISBN 978-1-64445-063-5 (paper)

2 4 6 8 9 7 5 3 1
First Graywolf Paperback, 2021

Library of Congress Control Number: 2020951350

Cover design: John Lucas

Cover art © Nona Faustine

You go down there looking for justice, that's what you find, just us.

When we define ourselves, when I define myself, the place in which I am like you and the place in which I am not like you, I am not excluding you from the joining—I am broadening the joining.

For Us

contents

JUST US

what if

i

What does it mean to want
an age-old call
for change
not to change

and yet, also,
to feel bullied
by the call to change?

How is a call to change named shame,
named penance, named chastisement?

How does one say

what if

without reproach? The root

of chastise is to make pure.
The impossibility of that—is that
what repels and not

the call for change?

ii

There is resignation in my voice when I say I feel
myself slowing down, gauging like a machine
the levels of my response. I remain within
so sore I think there is no other way than release—

so I ask questions like I know how
in the loneliness of my questioning.
What's still is true; there isn't even a tremor
when one is this historied out.

I could build a container to carry this being,
a container to hold all, though we were never
about completeness; we were never to be whole.

I stand in your considered thoughts also broken,
also unknown, extending
one sentence—here, I am here.
As I've known you, as I'll never know you,

I am here. Whatever is
being expressed, what if,
I am here awaiting, waiting for you

in the what if, in the questions,
in the conditionals,
in the imperatives—what if.

iii

What if over tea, what if on our walks, what if
in the long yawn of the fog, what if in the long middle
of the wait, what if in the passage, in the what if
that carries us each day into seasons, what if
in the renewed resilience, what if in the endlessness,
what if in a lifetime of conversations, what if
in the clarity of consciousness, what if nothing changes?

iv

What if you are responsible to saving more than to changing?

What if you're the destruction coursing beneath
your language of savior? Is that, too, not fucked up?

You say, if other white people had not . . . or if it seemed like
not enough . . . I would have . . .

What if—the repetitive call of what if—is only considered repetitive
when what if leaves my lips, when what if is uttered
by the unheard, and what if

what if is the cement of insistence
when you insist what if
this is.

v

What is it we want to keep conscious, to stay known, even as we
say, each in our own way, I so love I know I shrink I'm asked
I'm also I react I smell I feel I think I've been told I remember I
see I didn't I thought I felt I failed I suspect I was doing I'm sure
I read I needed I wouldn't I was I should've I felt I could've I
never I'm sure I ask . . .

You say and I say but what
is it we are telling, what is it

we are wanting to know about here?

vi

What if what I want from you is new, newly made
a new sentence in response to all my questions,

a swerve in our relation and the words that carry us,
the care that carries. I am here, without the shrug,
attempting to understand how what I want
and what I want from you run parallel—

justice and the openings for just us.

liminal spaces i

Text *What are Shirley Cards and how did they determine what was the correct skin tone balance?*

Notes and Sources Lorna Roth, "Looking at Shirley, the Ultimate Norm: Colour Balance, Image Technologies, and Cognitive Equity," *Canadian Journal of Communication*: "'Skin-colour balance' in still photography printing refers historically to a process in which a norm reference card showing a 'Caucasian' woman wearing a colourful, high-contrast dress is used as a basis for measuring and calibrating the skin tones on the photograph being printed. The light skin tones of these women—named 'Shirley' by male industry users after the name of the first colour test-strip-card model—have been the recognized skin ideal standard for most North American analogue photo labs since the early part of the twentieth century and they continue to function as the dominant norm."

See also Estelle Caswell, "Color Film Was Built for White People. Here's What It Did to Dark Skin," *Vox*, and Sarah Lewis, "The Racial Bias Built into Photography," the *New York Times*.

In the early days of the run-up to the 2016 election, I was just beginning to prepare a class on whiteness to teach at Yale University, where I had been newly hired. Over the years, I had come to realize that I often did not share historical knowledge with the persons to whom I was speaking. "What's redlining?" someone would ask. "George Washington freed his slaves?" someone else would inquire. What are Shirley Cards and how did they determine what was the correct skin tone balance? yet another person wondered. But as I listened to Donald Trump's inflammatory rhetoric during the campaign that spring, the class took on a new dimension. Would my students understand the long history that informed a comment like one Trump made when he announced his presidential candidacy? "When Mexico sends its people, they're not sending their best," he said. "They're sending people that have lots of problems, and they're bringing those problems with us. They're bringing drugs. They're bringing crime. They're rapists." When I heard those words, I wanted my students to track immigration laws in the United States. Would they connect the current treatment of both documented and undocumented Mexicans with the treatment of Irish, Italian, and Asian people in the last century?

In preparation, I needed to slowly unpack and understand how whiteness was created. How did the Naturalization Act of 1790, which restricted citizenship to "any alien, being a free white person," develop over the years into our various immigration acts? What has it taken to cleave citizenship from "free white person"? What was the trajectory of the Ku Klux Klan after its formation after the end of the Civil War, and what was its relationship to the Black Codes, those laws subsequently passed in Southern states to restrict black people's freedoms? Did the United States government bomb the black community in Tulsa, Oklahoma, also known as Black Wall

Text *"Given the seeming novelty of such white writing and the urgency of understanding white support for Ronald Reagan, 'critical whiteness studies' gained media attention and a small foothold in universities."*

Notes and Sources Daniel Wallis/Reuters, "Audio reveals Ronald Reagan calling African delegates 'monkeys'": "In a recently emerged audio recording from 1971, then-California Governor Ronald Reagan can be heard disparaging African delegates to the United Nations as 'monkeys' during a phone call with U.S. President Richard Nixon. . . . 'To see those monkeys from those African countries, damn them,' Reagan can be heard saying, prompting laughter from Nixon. 'They are still uncomfortable wearing shoes.'" In the 1984 presidential election, forty-nine of fifty states voted for Reagan.

& history repeats for Trump

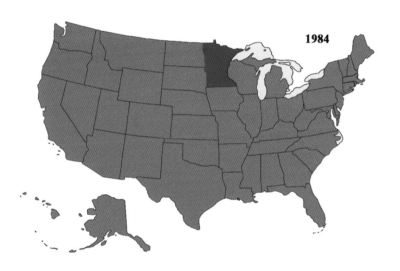

Street, in 1921? How did Italians, Irish, and Slavic peoples become white? Why do people believe abolitionists could not be racist?

I wanted my students to gain an awareness of a growing body of work by sociologists, theorists, historians, and literary scholars in a field known as "whiteness studies," the cornerstones of which include Toni Morrison's *Playing in the Dark: Whiteness and the Literary Imagination*, David Roediger's *The Wages of Whiteness*, Matthew Frye Jacobson's *Whiteness of a Different Color: European Immigrants and the Alchemy of Race*, Richard Dyer's *White*, and more recently Nell Irvin Painter's *The History of White People*. Roediger, a historian, had explained to me the development of the field, one that my class would engage with, saying, "The 1980s and early '90s saw the publication of major works on white identity's intricacies and costs by James Baldwin and Toni Morrison, alongside new works by white writers and activists asking similar questions historically. Given the seeming novelty of such white writing and the urgency of understanding white support for Ronald Reagan, 'critical whiteness studies' gained media attention and a small foothold in universities." This area of study aimed to make visible a history of whiteness that through its association with "normalcy" and "universality" masked its omnipresent institutional power.

My class eventually became Constructions of Whiteness, and over the two years that I have taught it, many of my students (who have included just about every race, gender identity, and sexual orientation) interviewed white people on campus or in their families about their understanding of American history and how it relates to whiteness. Some students simply wanted to know how others around them would define their own whiteness. Others were troubled by their own family members' racism and wanted to understand how and why certain prejudices formed.

Still others wanted to show the impact of white expectations on their lives.

Perhaps this is why one day in New Haven, staring into the semi-circle of oak trees in my backyard, I wondered what it would mean to ask random white men how they understood their privilege. I imagined myself—a middle-aged black woman—walking up to strangers to do so. Would they react as the police captain in Plainfield, Indiana, did when his female colleague told him during a diversity training session that he benefited from "white male privilege"? He became angry and accused her of using a racialized slur against him. (She was placed on paid administrative leave and a reprimand was placed in her file.) Would I, too, be accused? Would I hear myself asking about white male privilege and then watch white man after white man walk away as if I were mute? Would they think I worked for Trevor Noah, Stephen Colbert, or Chelsea Handler and just forgot my camera crew? The running comment in our current political climate is that we all need to converse with people we don't normally speak to, and though my husband is white, I found myself falling into easy banter with all kinds of strangers except white men. They rarely sought me out to shoot the breeze, and I did not seek them out. Maybe it was time to engage, even if my fantasies of these encounters seemed outlandish. I wanted to try.

Weeks later, it occurred to me that I tend to be surrounded by white men I don't know when I'm traveling, caught in places that are essentially nowhere: in between, en route, up in the air. As I crisscrossed the United States, Europe, and Africa giving talks about my work, I found myself considering these white men who passed hours with me in airport lounges, at gates, on planes. They seemed to me to make up the largest percentage of business

Text *Did he understand that, today, 64 percent of elected officials are white men, though they make up only 31 percent of the American population? White men have held almost all the power in this country for four hundred years.*

Fact Check Maybe. 62 percent and 30 percent are the updated numbers from the Reflective Democracy study. The study seems sound.

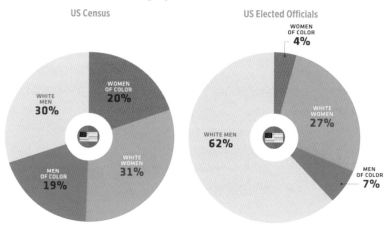

2019: Demographics of Political Power

US Census

US Elected Officials

Reflective Democracy Campaign

travelers in the liminal spaces where we waited. That I was among them in airport lounges and in first-class cabins spoke in part to my own relative economic privilege, but the price of my ticket, of course, does not translate into social capital. I was always aware that my value in our culture's eyes is determined by my skin color first and foremost. This is also true for the white men around me. Maybe these white male travelers could answer my questions about white privilege. I felt certain that, as a black woman, there had to be something I didn't understand.

Just recently, a friend who didn't get a job he applied for told me that, as a white male, he was absorbing the problems of the world. He meant he was being punished for the sins of his forefathers. He wanted me to know he understood it was his burden to bear. I wanted to tell him that he needed to take a long view of the history of the workplace, given the imbalances that generations of hiring practices before him had created. But would that really make my friend feel any better? Did he understand that, today, • 64 percent of elected officials are white men, though they make up only 31 percent of the American population? White men have held almost all the power in this country for four hundred years.

I knew that my friend was trying to communicate his struggle to find a way to understand the complicated American structure that holds us both. I wanted to ask him if his expectation was a sign of his privilege but decided, given the loss of his job opportunity, that my role as a friend probably demanded other responses.

After a series of casual conversations with my white male travelers, would I come to understand white privilege any differently? They couldn't know what it's like to be me, though who I am is in part a response to who they are, and I didn't really believe I understood them, even as they determined so much of what was possible in my

Traci Blackmon is ✈ traveling to Charlotte from Cleveland Hopkins International Airport (CLE).

🔊 **Follow**

May 4, 2019 · Cleveland, OH

#wheelsup
Standing in line to board.
I'm first in line.
A middle eastern man is second.
The line progresses from there.
Just before boarding a middle aged white woman struts up the side of me politely saying "excuse me" as she passes.

She then proceeded to position herself in front of me in line. To which I respond. Are you flying first class this afternoon. And she smiles and says "yes."

I respond: So am I. I am curious, if you don't mind me asking. What was it about me that caused you to presume I was not a first class passenger and therefore you should be in front of me.

Her face reddened. So I continued.

I thought perhaps it was my casual dress. I mean I'm wearing torn jeans and a tee. Perhaps you didn't think a person dressed this way would be in first class. But then I noticed you're wearing a baggy sweat suit. So it couldn't be that. I'm trying to figure out what it might be.

"I just didn't realize. I apologize," as she gathers herself and prepares to move. And then she proceeds to get behind me.

I look inquisitively at the Middle Eastern man. He shrugged his shoulders. So I said loudly: Sir, are you flying first class as well? I can't tell by looking at you. But I assume since you are standing here with me that you can read and you are in the place you should be.

Again. She gathers her bags, moves. And replies she didn't know.

A few minutes later. She comes back up to me to tell me how cute my shoes are. I imagine she realizes the error of her ways and wants me to know now that she indeed does see...my shoes.

I tell you.
This crap is exhausting.
But 👏 Every 👏 Time 👏 I 👏 Will 👏 Teach. 👏 You 👏 !!!!!!

I don't even like the whole first class thing. They gave it to me because of frequency. I ain't paying for it. But I may start. Just as an act of resistance!!!

 and 24 others   4 Comments 3 Shares

👍 Like   💬 Comment   ↪ Share

22

life and in the lives of others. But because I have only lived as me, a person who regularly has to negotiate conscious and unconscious dismissal, erasure, disrespect, and abuse, I fell into this wondering silently. Always, I hesitated.

I hesitated when I stood in line for a flight across the country, and a white man stepped in front of me. He was with another white man. "Excuse me," I said. "I am in this line." He stepped behind me but not before saying to his flight mate, "You never know who they're letting into first class these days."

Was his statement a defensive move meant to cover his rudeness and embarrassment, or were we sharing a joke? Perhaps he, too, had heard one of the many recent anecdotes on social media in which a black woman recalled a white woman's stepping in front of her at her gate. In one when the black woman told her she was in line, the white woman responded that it was the line for first class. In another she simply says "excuse me" and inserts herself in front of the black woman. Was the man's comment a sly reference? But he wasn't laughing, not even a little. Deadpan.

Later, when I discussed this moment with my therapist, she told me that she thought the man's statement was in response to his flight

HA! yes,
reveal him

Daughter of Black Woman: "Don't you
dare shout at her."

White Man: "Don't tell me what to do.
If I tell her to get out, she gets out."

Daughter of Black Woman: "No she
won't! Can you [flight attendant] sort
him out, you know it's rude to talk to
her like that, who the hell are you, you
old tramp."

White Man: "I'll tell you I hope
somebody sits there because I don't
want to sit next to your sickly face,
your ugly fucking face."

Flight Attendant: "Excuse me lady,
excuse me ma'am, do you want to sit
in another seat?"

White Man: "Put her to another seat.
It's only polite to get out. I can't get in
my seat" [inaudible].

Black Woman: [to flight attendant]
"That's all right, that's all right, that's
okay. [to unnamed white man] You
smell, you need a wash."

White Man: "I'll tell you this, if you
don't go to another seat, I'll push you
to another seat."

Passenger in the Row Behind: "Stop,
stop, stop."

Passenger in the Row Behind: "Just
don't even bother speaking to each
other."

White Man: [to woman] "Don't talk to
me in a fucking foreign language, you
stupid ugly cow."

Passenger in the Row Behind: "Mate,
will you stop."

White Man: "I will carry on as far as I
can with this ugly black bastard."

mate, not me. I didn't matter to him, she said; that's why he could step in front of me in the first place. His embarrassment, if it was embarrassment, had everything to do with how he was seen by the person who did matter: his white male companion. I was allowing myself to have too much presence in his imagination, she said. Should this be a comfort? Was my total invisibility preferable to a targeted insult?

During the flight, each time he removed or replaced something in his case overhead, he looked over at me. Each time, I looked up from my book to meet his gaze and smiled—I like to think I'm not humorless. I tried to imagine what my presence was doing to him. On some level, I thought, I must have dirtied up his narrative of white privilege securing white spaces. In my class, I had taught "Whiteness as Property," an article published in the *Harvard Law Review* in 1993, in which the author, Cheryl Harris, argues that "the set of assumptions, privileges, and benefits that accompany the status of being white have become a valuable asset that whites sought to protect." These are the assumptions of privilege and exclusion that have led many white Americans to call the police on black people trying to enter their own homes or vehicles. Racial profiling becomes another sanctioned method of segregating space. Harris goes on to explain how much white people rely on these benefits, so much so that their expectations inform the interpretations of our laws. "Stand your ground" laws, for example, mean whites can claim that fear made them kill an unarmed black person.

The same fear defense has allowed many police who kill unarmed blacks to continue working and then retire with their pensions. Or voter registration laws in certain states can function as de facto Jim Crow laws. "American law," Harris writes, "has recognized a property interest in whiteness."

Text *The phrase "white privilege" was popularized in 1988 by Peggy McIntosh, a Wellesley College professor who wanted to define "invisible systems conferring racial dominance on my group."*

Fact Check Yes. The term was put in circulation prior to McIntosh.

Notes and Sources Theodore W. Allen was conducting an analysis of what he variously called "white skin privilege," "white racial privilege," and "white privilege" in the 1960s, '70s, and '80s. See his text *The Invention of the White Race*. For a thorough discussion of the term's use prior to McIntosh, see Jacob Bennett, "White Privilege: A History of the Concept" (master's thesis, Georgia State University, 2012), https://scholarworks.gsu.edu/history_theses/54.

On the plane, I wanted to enact a new narrative that included the whiteness of the man who had stepped in front of me. I felt his whiteness should be a component of what we both understood about him, even as his whiteness would not be the entirety of who he is. His unconscious understanding of whiteness meant the space I inhabited should have been only his. The old script would have left his whiteness unacknowledged in my consideration of his slight. But a rude man and a rude white man have different presumptions. Just as when a white person confronted by an actual black human being needs to negotiate stereotypes of blackness so that they can arrive at the person standing before them, I hoped to give the man the same courtesy but in the reverse. Seeing his whiteness meant I understood my presence as an unexpected demotion for him. It was too bad if he felt that way. Still, I wondered, what is this "stuckness" inside racial hierarchies that refuses the neutrality of the skies? I hoped to find a way to have this conversation.

The phrase "white privilege" was popularized in 1988 by Peggy McIntosh, a Wellesley College professor who wanted to define "invisible systems conferring racial dominance on my group." McIntosh came to understand that she benefited from hierarchical assumptions and policies simply because she was white. I would have preferred if instead of "white privilege" she had used the term "white living," because "privilege" suggested white dominance was tied to economics. Nonetheless, the phrase has stuck. The title of her essay "White Privilege and Male Privilege: A Personal Account of Coming to See Correspondences through Work in Women's Studies" was a mouthful. McIntosh listed forty-six ways white privilege is enacted. "Number 19: I can speak in public to a powerful male group without putting my race on trial"; "Number 20: I can do well in a challenging situation without being called a credit to my race"; "Number 27: I

[handwritten margin note: What's the point of ● < 14.3?]

[handwritten margin note: I disagree 'privilege' has evolved]

can go home from most meetings of organizations I belong to feeling somewhat tied in, rather than isolated, out-of-place, out-numbered, unheard, held at a distance or feared"; "Number 36: If my day, week or year is going badly, I need not ask of each negative episode or situation whether it had racial overtones." I'm not clear why McIntosh stopped at 46 except as a way of saying, "You get the picture." Students were able to add their own examples easily.

My students and I also studied the work of the white documentary filmmaker Whitney Dow. In the past couple of years, Dow has been part of Columbia University's Interdisciplinary Center for Innovative Theory and Empirics (INCITE), which gathered data on more than 850 people, the vast majority of whom identified as white or partly white and the communities in which they lived. He filmed more than a hundred of their oral histories. This work, like McIntosh's, was another way of thinking about the ordinariness of white hierarchical thinking. I asked Dow what he learned in his conversations with white men. "They are struggling to construct a just narrative for themselves as new information comes in, and they are having to restructure and re-fashion their own narratives and coming up short," he said. "I include myself in that," he added after a moment. "We are seeing the deconstruction of the white-male archetype. The individual actor on the grand stage always had the support of a genocidal government, but this is not the narrative we grew up with. It's a challenge to adjust." *→not to adjust, but to accept*

Is this why? no, they are having trouble b/c the narrative is something they want to avoid

The interviews, collected in INCITE's initial report, *Facing Whiteness*, which is accessible on Columbia University's website, vary greatly in terms of knowledge of American history and experiences. One interviewee declares: "The first slave owner in America was a

Excerpted from a conversation between Manthia Diawara and Édouard Glissant aboard the *Queen Mary II* (August 2009)

Manthia Diawara

We're travelling aboard the *Queen Mary II*, on our way to New York from Southampton. Why a ship, when it would have been easier and faster to travel on a plane?

Édouard Glissant

Ever since I started having heart trouble, I've been unable to take long-distance flights. And since it's eight and a half hours from Paris to Fort-de-France, I'm obliged to take the boat, and this one is pretty much the only one that makes regular trips. It's all quite ambiguous, because you'd think that a boat is a sign of comfort and ease, but in my opinion it's quite the opposite. It's a sign of catching up the time lost; the time that you cannot let slip away or run away, the times that you become caught up in things—you can't flee or run anywhere. It seems to me that on any kind of boat you can be closer to yourself, while in a plane you're really detached from yourself—you're not yourself, you're something else. And I'm saying this jokingly—and I'm not alone in this—it's not normal for a person to be suspended in the air even if man's always dreamed of being a bird. Accordingly, I take this boat regularly when I have to go to Martinique or New York. . . .

MD A boat connotes a departure from point A and an arrival at point B—in this context, it is a departure for the Africans who are captured for the first time and pushed onto a boat. What does departure mean to you?

ÉG It's the moment when one consents not to be a single being and attempts to be many beings at the same time. In other words, for me every diaspora is the passage from unity to multiplicity. I think that's what's important in all the movements of the world, and we, the descendants, who have arrived from the other shore, would be wrong to cling fiercely to this singularity which had accepted to go out into the world. Let us not forget that Africa has been the source of all kinds of diasporas—not only the forced diaspora imposed by the West through the slave trade, but also of millions of all types of diasporas before—that have populated the world. One of Africa's vocations is to be a kind of foundational Unity which develops and transforms itself into a Diversity. And it seems to me that, if we don't think about that properly, we won't be able to understand what we ourselves can do, as participants in this African diaspora, to help the world to realise its true self, in other words its multiplicity, and to respect itself as such.

beautiful

black man. How many people know that? The slaves that were brought to America were sold to the white man by blacks. So, I don't feel that we owe them any special privileges other than that anybody else has, any other race." While this interviewee denies any privilege, another has come to see how his whiteness enables his mobility in America: "I have to accept the reality that because I'm a man, I—whether I was aware of that or not at any specific time—probably had some sort of hand up in a situation." He added, "The longer I'm in law enforcement and the more aware I am of the world around me, the more I realize that being of Anglo-Saxon descent, being a man and being in a region of America that is somewhat rural, and because it's rural by default mostly white, means that I definitely get preference." This interviewee, according to Dow, had been "pretty ostracized because of his progressiveness" in the workplace. While he recognizes his privilege, he still indicates, through his use of words like "probably" and phrases like "because it's rural by default mostly white," that he believes white privilege is in play in only certain circumstances. Full comprehension would include the understanding that white privilege comes with expectations of protection and preferences no matter where he lives in the country, what job he has, or how much money he makes.

How angry could I be at the white man on the plane, the one who glanced at me each time he stood up the way you look at a stone you had tripped on? I understood that the man's behavior was also his socialization. My own socialization had, in many ways, prepared me for him. I was not overwhelmed by our encounter because my blackness is consent "not to be a single being." This phrase, which finds its origins in the work of the West Indian writer Édouard Glissant but was reintroduced to me in the recent work of the poet and critical theorist Fred Moten, gestures toward the fact that I can refuse the white man's stereotypes of blackness,

even as he interacts with those stereotypes. What I wanted was to know what the white man saw or didn't see when he walked in front of me at the gate.

It's hard to exist and also accept my lack of existence. Frank Wilderson III, chair of African American Studies at the University of California, Irvine, borrows from Orlando Patterson the sociological term "social death" to explain my there-but-not-there status in a historically antiblack society. The outrage—and if we are generous, the embarrassment that occasioned the white passenger's comment—was a reaction to the unseen taking up space; space itself is one of the understood privileges of whiteness.

but also asian? arguably equally erased

Before the airlines decided frequent travelers need not stand in line, a benefit now afforded to me, I was waiting in another line for access to another plane in another city as another group of white men approached. When they realized they would have to get behind a dozen or so people already in line, they simply formed their own line next to us. I said to the white man standing in front of me, "Now, that is the height of white male privilege." He laughed and remained smiling all the way to his seat. He wished me a good flight. We had shared something. I don't know if it was the same thing for each of us—the same recognition of racialized being in the world—but I could live with that polite form of unintelligibility.

I found the suited men who refused to fall in line exhilarating and amusing (as well as obnoxious). Watching them was like watching a spontaneous play about white male privilege in one act. I appreciated the drama. One or two of them chuckled at their own audacity. The gate agent did an interesting sort of check-in by merging the newly formed line with the actual line. The people in my line, almost all white and male themselves, were in turn

roxane gay ✔
@rgay

Following ⌄

Man behind me is loudly speculating as to whether or not I am supposed to be in the sky prioroty line. And I saw his boarding pass. We are not in the same section of the plane, ahem.

7:07 AM - 29 Dec 2018

106 Retweets **5,484** Likes

💬 101   🔁 106   ♡ 5.5K   ✉

Tweet your reply

Barry Jenkins ✔ @BarryJenkins · 23h
Replying to @rgay
All. De. Damn. Time.

💬 1   🔁 2   ♡ 292   ✉

quizzical and accepting. After I watched this scene play out, I filed it away to use as an example in my class. How would my students read this moment? Some would no doubt be enraged by the white female gate agent who let it happen. I would ask why it was easier to be angry with her than with the group of men. Because she doesn't recognize or utilize her institutional power, someone would say. Based on past classes, I could assume the white male students would be quick to distance themselves from the men at the gate; white solidarity has no place in a class that sets out to make visible the default positions of whiteness.

As the professor, I felt this was a narrative that could help me gauge the level of recognition of white privilege in the class, because other white people were also inconvenienced by the actions of this group of men. The students wouldn't be distracted by society's "abuse of minorities" because everyone seemed inconvenienced. Some students, though, would want to see the moment as gendered, not racialized. I would ask them if they could imagine a group of black men pulling off this action without the white men in my line responding or the gate agent questioning the men even if they were within their rights.

As I became more and more frustrated with myself for avoiding asking my question, I wondered if presumed segregation in one's white life should have been number 47 on McIntosh's list. Just do it, I told myself. Just ask a random white guy how he feels about his privilege.

On my next flight, I came close. I was a black woman in the company of mostly white men, in seats that allowed for both proximity and separate spaces. The flight attendant brought drinks to everyone around me but repeatedly forgot my orange juice. Telling

Is how you are treated @ airplanes really the prism to understand white privilege + feels superficial

Does Rankine ever see the privilege of her own? That there's a layer of capitalist underture here

35

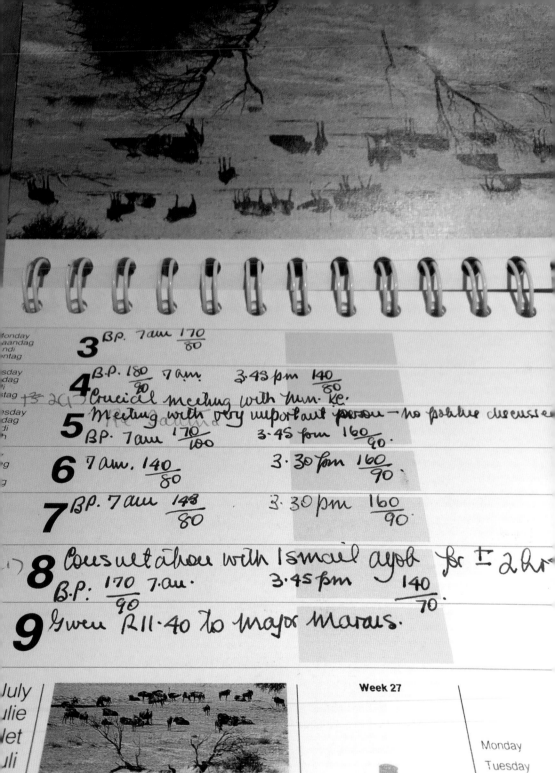

Monday Maandag Mandi Montag	**3** B.P. 7am $\frac{170}{80}$
Tuesday Dinsdag ...	**4** B.P. 180 7am. 3.45 pm $\frac{140}{80}$ $\frac{90}$ +3 2b? Crucial meeting with Min. Ke.
Wednesday Woensdag ...	**5** Meeting with very important person — no politics discusse B.P. 7am $\frac{170}{100}$ 3.45 pm $160\frac{}{90}$.
... ...	**6** 7am. $\frac{140}{80}$ 3.30 pm $\frac{160}{90}$
	7 B.P. 7am $\frac{148}{80}$ 3.30 pm $160\frac{}{90}$
	8 Consultation with Ismail ayob for ± 2 hr B.P. $\frac{170}{90}$ 7.am. 3.45 pm $\frac{140}{70}$.
	9 Given R11.40 to major Marais.

July
Julie
Jwet
Juli

Week 27

Monday
Tuesday
Wednesday
Thursday
Friday
Saturday

myself orange juice is sugar and she might be doing my post-cancer body a favor, I just nodded when she apologized for the second time. The third time she walked by without the juice, the white man sitting next to me said to her, "This is incredible. You have brought me two drinks in the time you have forgotten to bring her one."

She returned immediately with the juice.

I thanked him. He said, "She isn't suited to her job." I didn't respond, "She didn't forget your drinks. She didn't forget you. You are seated next to no one in this no place." Instead, I said, "She just likes you more." He perhaps thought I was speaking about him in particular and blushed. Did he understand I was joking about being white in the world? It didn't seem so. The red crept up his neck into his cheeks, and he looked shy and pleased at the same time. He brought both hands up to his face as if to hold in the heat of this embarrassing pleasure.

"Coming or going?" he asked, changing the subject.

"I'm returning from Johannesburg."

"Really?" he said. "I was just in Cape Town."

Hence your advocacy, I thought ungenerously.

Why was that thought in my head? I myself am overdetermined by my race. Is that avoidable? Is that a problem? Had I made the problem or was I given the problem? I think of Nelson Mandela's blood pressure (BP) rising to 170 over 100 on a day he purportedly met with Frederik Willem de Klerk. Hearsay or fact? Who knows.

LOL

37

As I looked at the man in seat 2B, I wondered if my historical po-
sitioning was turning his humanity into evidence of white male
dominance. Are white men overdetermined by their skin color in
my eyes? Are they being forced, as my friend suggested, to absorb
the problems of the world?

I wonder this too

On the long flight, I didn't bring up white male privilege, jokes or
otherwise, again. Instead we wandered around our recent memo-
ries of South Africa and discussed the resort where he stayed
and the safari I took. I didn't bring up Soweto or the Apartheid
Museum that I visited in Johannesburg or the lynching memorial
in Montgomery, Alabama, which the Apartheid Museum reminded
me of. I wanted my fellow traveler to begin a conversation about
his whiteness this time. For once. I wanted him to think about
his whiteness, especially because he had just left South Africa,
a country that suffered, as James Baldwin said, "from the same
delusion the Americans suffer from—it too thought it was a white
country." But I imagined he felt the less said about race relations
in the United States or South Africa, the more possible it was for
us to be interlocutors. That was my fantasy, in any case.

Back home, when I mentioned these encounters to my white
husband, he was amused. "They're just defensive," he said. "White
fragility," he added, with a laugh. This white man who has spent
the past twenty-five years in the world alongside me believes
he understands and recognizes his own privilege. Certainly he
knows the right terminology to use, even when these agreed-
upon terms prevent us from stumbling into moments of real rec-
ognition. These phrases—white fragility, white defensiveness,
white appropriation—have a habit of standing in for the compli-
cated mess of a true conversation. At that moment, he wanted to
discuss our current president instead. "That," he said, "is a clear

case of indignation and rage in the face of privilege writ large. Real power. Real consequences." He was not wrong, of course, but he joined all the "woke" white men who set their privilege outside themselves—as in, I know better than to be ignorant or defensive about my status in our world. Never mind that that capacity to set himself outside the pattern of white male dominance is the privilege. It, perhaps, brings them comfort. White comfort. There's no outrunning the kingdom, the power, and the glory.

I finally got up my nerve to ask a stranger directly about white privilege as I was sitting next to him at the gate. He had initiated our conversation, because he was frustrated about yet another delay. We shared that frustration together. Eventually he asked what I did, and I told him that I write and teach. "Where do you teach?" he asked. "Yale," I answered. He told me his son wanted to go there but hadn't been accepted during the early-application process. "It's tough when you can't play the diversity card," he added.

Was he thinking out loud? Were the words just slipping out before he could catch them? Was this the innocence of white privilege? Was he yanking my chain? Was he snapping the white-privilege flag in my face? Should I have asked him why he had the expectation that his son should be admitted early, without delay, without pause, without waiting? Should I have asked how he knew a person of color "took" his son's seat and not another white son of one of these many white men sitting around us?

I was perhaps holding my breath. I decided to just breathe.

"The Asians are flooding the Ivy Leagues," he added after a moment. Perhaps the clarification was intended to make it clear that

41

Text *The historian Matthew Frye Jacobson, in* Whiteness of a Different Color, *describes the twentieth century's reconsolidating of the nineteenth century's "Celts, Hebrews, Teutons, Mediterraneans and Slavs."*

Notes and Sources Jacobson traces immigration history and policies from the second half of the nineteenth century, when "white" Europeans were cataloged by their distinct racial types, to the early to mid-twentieth century, when perceived differences of those same racial distinctions declined dramatically. Frye writes, "Immigration restriction, along with internal black migrations, altered the nation's racial alchemy and redrew the dominant racial configuration along the strict, binary line of white and black, creating Caucasians where before had been so many Celts, Hebrews, Teutons, Mediterraneans and Slavs."

Text *I asked if he gets flagged by TSA. "Not usually," he said.*

Notes and Sources See the April 17, 2019, article on ProPublica, "TSA Agents Say They're Not Discriminating against Black Women, but Their Body Scanners Might Be": "Black women have been raising alarms for years about being forced to undergo intrusive, degrading searches of their hair at airport security checkpoints. After a complaint five years ago, the TSA pledged to improve oversight and training for its workers on hair pat-downs. But it turns out there's an issue beyond the screeners: the machines themselves."

he wasn't speaking right now about his fantasies regarding black people and affirmative action. He had remembered something. He had recalled who was sitting next to him.

Then I did it. I asked. "I've been thinking about white male privilege, and I wonder if you think about yours or your son's?" It almost seemed to be a non sequitur, but he rolled with it.

"Not me," he said. "I've worked hard for everything I have."

What was it that Justice Brett Kavanaugh said at his Supreme Court confirmation hearing? "I got into Yale Law School. That's the number one law school in the country. I had no connections there. I got there by busting my tail in college." He apparently believed this despite the fact that his grandfather went to Yale. I couldn't tell by looking at this man I was sitting next to, but I wondered if he was an ethnic white rather than a white Anglo-Saxon Protestant. The historian Matthew Frye Jacobson, in *Whiteness of a Different Color*, describes the twentieth century's reconsolidating of the nineteenth century's "Celts, Hebrews, Teutons, Mediterraneans and Slavs." By the 1940s, according to David Roediger, "given patterns of intermarriage across ethnicity and Cold War imperatives," whites stopped dividing hierarchically within whiteness and begin identifying as socially constructed Caucasians.

I said to the man, "What if I said I wasn't referring to generations of economic wealth, to *Mayflower* wealth and connections?" I was speaking instead of simply living. I asked if he gets flagged by TSA. "Not usually," he said. "I have Global Entry."

"So do I," I said, "but I still get stopped." The "randomness" of racial profiling is a phenomenon I could talk about forever, but I

Text *The word "home" turned him back to his son. He said his son's best friend was Asian and had been admitted to Yale on early action or early decision or early admissions.*

Notes and Sources See Anemona Hartocollis and Stephanie Saul, "Affirmative Action Battle Has a New Focus: Asian-Americans," in the *New York Times*: "A Princeton study found that students who identify as Asian need to score 140 points higher on the SAT than whites to have the same chance of admission to private colleges, a difference some have called 'the Asian tax.'"

Evidence for white advantage in elite admissions processes is elite institutions' preference for legacy students, recruited athletes, and children of faculty. Daniel Golden's ProPublica article, published in July 2018, "How the Fight against Affirmative Action at Harvard Could Threaten Rich Whites," examines how these special categories give certain white applicants a leg up at Harvard. Golden reports that children of Harvard alumni comprise 21.5 percent of accepted white applicants, and only 7 percent of those identified as Hispanic, 6.6 percent of Asian Americans, and 4.8 percent of African Americans. Golden writes that, according to Duke economist Peter Arcidiacono, "Overall, across six years, Harvard accepted 33.6 percent of legacy applicants, versus 5.9 percent of non-legacies."

Golden also reports that "recruited athletes get the biggest edge of all, with an 86-percent acceptance rate. They comprise 16.3 percent of white students who are admitted to Harvard, as against 8.9 percent of blacks, 4.2 percent of Hispanics, and 4.1 percent of Asian Americans."

Golden notes too that Harvard accepted 46.7 percent of the children of Harvard faculty and staff.

stopped myself that day. "Are you able to move in and out of public spaces without being questioned as to why you are there?" I asked. "Do people rush forward asking how they can help you?" I knew the answer to my questions, but I asked them anyway, because I wanted to slow down a dynamic he benefited from.

He said he saw my point. I wanted to say, "It's not my point, it's our reality," but the declarative nature of the sentence felt sharp on my tongue. I wanted to keep talking with this man, and I knew my race and gender meant he was wary of me and my questions—questions that might lead to the word "racist" or "sexist." If only skin color didn't have such predictive power.

I didn't want our different historical positioning to drown our already shipwrecked chat. I wanted to learn something that surprised me about this stranger, something I couldn't have known beforehand. Then it hit me. There wasn't enough time to develop trust, but everyone likes a listener. "Coming or going?" is the traveler's neutral, nonprying question. So now I asked him. He was heading home.

The word "home" turned him back to his son. He said his son's best friend was Asian and had been admitted to Yale on early action or early decision or early admissions. Neither of us knew the terminology. I wondered how he comforted his son. Had he used "the diversity card" as he had with me? I didn't want to discuss college admissions policy anymore. I wanted our conversation to go down any other road, but I had somehow become a representative of Yale, not a stranger sitting next to another stranger.

I reminded myself that I was there only to listen. Just listen. The man was deeply earnest and obviously felt helpless about the uncertainty of his son's future. But it couldn't be too dismal if Yale

was still an option. Don't think, I reminded myself. Know what it is to parent. Know what it is to love. Know what it is to be white. Know what it is to expect what white people could have whether or not luck or economics allow you to have it. Know what it is to resent. Is that unfair? Resentment has no home here. Know what it is to be white. Is that ungenerous? I don't know. Don't think.

I didn't ask this white man why he thought his son was any more entitled to a place at Yale than his son's Asian friend. I didn't want him to feel he needed to defend his son's worth or his son's intelligence to me. I wanted his son to thrive. I did. Were his son to arrive in my class, I would help him do his best. The more he achieved at Yale, the more pleased I would be for both of us. If his son told the class he got into Yale because many of his white teachers from kindergarten on exaggerated his intelligence, I would interrupt him, as I have done in the past, and say, "No, you got into Yale and you have the capacity to understand that many factors contributed to your acceptance."

College admissions processes can't be discussed in definitive ways; they're full of gray areas, and those gray areas are often white-leaning, even as plenty of whites are denied entrance. We know that. I was suddenly reluctant to have a conversation about white-perceived spaces and entitlement or, God forbid, affirmative action, which would of course flood the space between us with black and brown people, me included. I said instead, "Wherever your son goes will work out, and in five years none of this will matter." It was in this moment that I recognized my exhaustion. And then came the realization that we were, in fact, in the midst of a discussion about the perceived loss of white male privilege, which in other words is simply a white life in which no one died. Was I implicated in his loss? Did he think so?

47

Text *This is a statement for well-meaning white people whose privilege and blind desire catapult them into a time when little black children and little white children are judged not "by the color of their skin but by the content of their character."*

Fact Check Examples of colorblind rhetoric below.

Notes and Sources Supreme Court judge John Harlan's early invocation of color blindness in *Plessy v. Ferguson*: "The white race deems itself to be the dominant race in this country. And so it is, in prestige, in achievements, in education, in wealth, and in power. So, I doubt not, it will continue to be for all time, if it remains true to its great heritage and holds fast to the principles of constitutional liberty. But in the view of the Constitution, in the eye of the law, there is in this country no superior, dominant, ruling class of citizens. There is no caste here. Our Constitution is color-blind, and neither knows nor tolerates classes among citizens. In respect of civil rights, all citizens are equal before the law."

Former Republican Party chairman and George H. W. Bush's 1988 campaign manager Lee Atwater's allusions to "colorblind racial ideology" during a taped interview in 1981 (quoted in *Colorblind Racial Profiling: A History, 1974 to the Present* by Guy Padula): "Here's how I would handle that issue . . . as a psychologist, which I am not, is how abstract you handle the race thing. You start out, I don't want you to quote me on this, you start out in 1954 by saying, 'Nigger, nigger, nigger.' By 1968 you can't say 'nigger'—that hurts you, backfires. So you say stuff like, uh, forced busing, states' rights, and all that stuff, and you're getting so abstract. Now, you're talking about cutting taxes, and all these things you're talking about are totally economic things and a byproduct of them is, blacks get hurt worse than whites. . . . 'We want to cut this,' is much more abstract than even the busing thing, uh, and a hell of a lot more abstract than 'Nigger, nigger.'"

Not long after this, I was on another flight and sitting next to a white man who felt as if he could already be a friend. Our conversation had the ease of kicking a ball around on a fall afternoon. Or it felt like stepping out the door in late spring when suddenly the temperature inside and out reads the same on your skin. Resistance falls away; your shoulders relax. I was, metaphorically, happily outdoors with this man, who was open and curious with a sense of humor. He spoke about his wife and sons with palpable affection. And though he was with me on the plane, he was there with them as well. His father was an academic, his mother a great woman.

a poet indeed

He asked who my favorite musician was, and I told him the Commodores because of one song, "Nightshift," which is basically an elegy. He loved Bruce Springsteen, but "Nightshift" was also one of his favorite songs. We sang lyrics from "Nightshift" together: "I still can hear him say, 'Aw, talk to me so you can see what's going on.'" When he asked if I knew a certain song by Springsteen, I admitted I didn't. I could only think of "American Skin (41 Shots)": "No secret, my friend, you can get killed just for living in your American skin." I knew those lyrics, but I didn't start singing them. I made a mental note to check out the Springsteen song he loved.

Eventually, he told me he had been working on diversity inside his company. "We still have a long way to go," he said. Then he repeated himself—"We still have a long way to go"—adding, "I don't see color." This is a statement for well-meaning white people whose privilege and blind desire catapult them into a time when little black children and little white children are judged not "by the color of their skin but by the content of their character." The phrase "I don't see color" pulled an emergency brake in my brain. Would you be bringing up diversity if you didn't see color?

Let's face it. I am a marked woman, but not everybody knows my name.

Hortense J. Spillers

Just when I start thinking I've been underestimated a lot in my career, I remember that I've still always been a giant white dude whenever I walked into the room.

I never once was made to feel like I didn't belong somewhere (even when I really didn't belong places).

Alexis Ohanian

I wondered. Will you tell your wife you had a nice talk with a woman or a black woman? Help.

All I could think to say was "Ain't I a black woman?" I asked the question slowly, as if testing the air quality. Did he get the riff on Sojourner Truth? Or did he think the ungrammatical construction was a sign of blackness? Or did he think I was mocking white people's understanding of black intelligence? "Aren't you a white man?" I then asked. "Can't you see that? Because if you can't see race, you can't see racism." I repeated that sentence, which I read not long before in Robin DiAngelo's *White Fragility*.

"I get it," he said. His tone was solemn. "What other inane things have I said?"

"Only that," I responded.

I had refused to let the reality he was insisting on be my reality. And I was pleased that I hadn't lubricated the moment, pleased I could say no to the silencing mechanisms of manners, pleased he didn't need to open up a vein of complaint. I was pleased he was not passively bullying. I was pleased he could carry the disturbance of my reality. And just like that, we broke open our conversation—random, ordinary, exhausting, and full of longing to exist in some image of less segregated spaces.

Not long after this exchange the man on the flight got in touch with me. He and his wife had read one of my books and we planned to get together. Our schedules, however, never worked out and time passed. Then I wrote the piece about speaking with white men about their privilege and I sent it to him. I didn't want to publish it without letting him know I had recounted our

conversation. I then asked him if he would respond to what I had written. He wrote back:

When you challenged me on my "I don't see color" comment, I understood your point, appreciated your candor, thought about it, and realized you were right. I saw your response as an act of both courage and generosity.

I've thought a lot about our conversation since that flight. In fact, not long afterwards I realized that I had misrepresented something I'd said to you about my hometown. I don't know why. I certainly hadn't done it intentionally, and I believed I was being honest in the moment. But after our talk, it was evident. I told you I didn't notice much tension between the black kids and the white kids in our town (I grew up and went through the public-school system of a middle-class suburb in the Northeast in the 1980s and early 1990s). I guess it's not that I didn't notice it so much as I wanted to forget it, because thinking back, tension was everywhere. I graduated from high school more than 25 years ago, and, except for college summers and a few months after graduation, haven't lived there since. Maybe it was such a constant in our lives that I didn't think about it— except for the overtly ugly incidents, like the time the white kid who sat in front of me in freshman algebra turned around and asked if I were planning to go to the varsity basketball game that night to watch "the [racial slur] play." I remember only a couple of physical fights between black kids and white kids, but cruelty, from mostly white to black, was always only a comment away. My home and my family (even my extended family, who were first and second generation from Mediterranean and Eastern European countries) were the antithesis of that type of behavior. But thinking back, it was all around us. It's interesting that something in our conversation made me realize it.

As I read and reread this response, I realized I had accepted what he said about his childhood hometown not as the truth but as

Ruby Sales

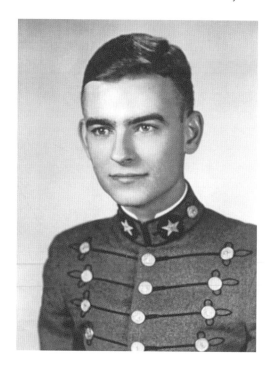

Jonathan Daniels

the truth about his whiteness. I had accepted it as the truth, as social justice activist Ruby Sales would say, about the "culture of whiteness." The lack of an integrated life meant that no part of his life recognized the treatment of black people as an important disturbance. To not remember is perhaps not to feel touched by events that don't interfere with your livelihood. This is the reality that defines white privilege no matter how much money one has or doesn't have. From Appalachia to Fifth Avenue, my precarity is not a reality shared. Though my seatmate misrepresented the fact of the matter, he did not misrepresent the role those facts played in his own life. I don't doubt that he believed what he said at the time. And in the days that followed our conversation, I don't doubt the repressed reality began pushing at the fiction of the facts, which is also in its way a truth. To let me in was to let in the disturbance of racial relations in a lifetime of segregated whiteness. If white people keep forgetting to remember that black lives matter, as they clearly do given their acceptance of everything from racist comments by friends and colleagues to the lack of sentencing of most police officers who kill unarmed blacks, to more structural racist practices, then they will always be surprised when those memories take hold.

evolution

Text *Awareness has to happen in rooms where everyone's white, since those rooms are already in place.*

Fact Check Yes, see sources on segregation below.

Notes and Sources For "rooms where everyone's white," see the *Washington Post* report by Chris Ingraham, "Three Quarters of Whites Don't Have Any Non-White Friends," on a study that found that 75 percent of white people have "entirely white social networks without any minority presence." According to a 2017 Pew report, the rate at which white newlyweds marry other white people was 89 percent. Entire counties exist that are almost 100 percent white. Another recent Pew study found that "most black and Asian adults (63% and 66%, respectively) say race or race relations come up in their conversations with family and friends at least sometimes, compared with about half of white (50%) and Hispanic (49%) adults." For an overview of recent data on spatial segregation in the United States, see this *Washington Post* report: "America Is More Diverse Than Ever—but Still Segregated."

From a historical perspective, the effects of long-standing segregationist policies and laws at the federal, state, and local levels are still felt and seen today. According to Richard Rothstein's *The Color of Law* in regard to housing, current residential segregation "is not the unintended consequence of individual choices . . . but of unhidden public policy that explicitly segregated every metropolitan area in the United States." Rothstein maintains that even without such government-mandated racial segregation, "other causes—private prejudice, white flight, real estate steering, bank redlining, income differences, and self-segregation—still would have existed but with far less opportunity for expression."

A black friend says white people are taking over antiracism work. Is he serious? He doesn't mean it just economically. He's not being asked to run diversity workshops when white spaces can get white women to do that. I ask jokingly, isn't that what black and brown people have been asking for? "It's not my job to educate white folks"—isn't that a statement I've heard numerous times? But like my friend, I feel race relations and differences are more complicated than simply an ignorant dynamic I resent being party to. We all feel we know what's up but can we, for all our entanglement, truly know what motivates the other? I do know my life, livelihood, and life possibilities depend on knowing more of certain things that white people willfully ignore. Who will represent that reality if a black person isn't in the room? I see my friend's point.

Later that same day I ask a white friend about white people speaking among themselves about their racism. It doesn't happen, she tells me. Nonetheless, she believes, that's how whites would learn to build stamina regarding their collusion with structural racism. The least of it are the daily infractions whites commit by saying and doing regrettable things, given their socialization in a culture that is set up to keep them ignorant of their ignorance of the violence committed against people of color, whether by policy, exception, surveillance, or neglect. Their socialization fundamentally affects people of color, whether or not individual whites are present for the institutionalization of racist decisions and omissions.

Because decisions get made that reinstate white hierarchies every day, it would be good if the culture of whiteness were marked and made visible to those who can't see it by those not invested in keeping it primary. Awareness has to happen in rooms where everyone's white, since those rooms are already in place.

Text *Aren't these conversations, which are ostensibly attempts to work on whiteness without reinstating white hierarchical thinking, choosing white comfort over white discomfort and integration? Is that a problem?*

Notes and Sources For an extended argument for integration, see the philosopher Elizabeth Anderson's *The Imperative of Integration.*

Scenario:

o While teaching a section on African Art you display the following image and ask students what they think of the image. A student states that the image "looks like a monkey." Some students in the class laugh at the response and some Black students look upset.

o What are your thoughts about this comment?

o How might you respond to this situation?

But, I tell my friend, I think it's ironic that conversations allowing whites to speak openly about whiteness should start within segregated spaces. Aren't these conversations, which are ostensibly attempts to work on whiteness without reinstating white hierarchical thinking, choosing white comfort over white discomfort and integration? Is that a problem? Cognition formation is in part influenced by environment.

My friend says this is a "stark" way to look at it. But if you're white and you're getting messages from your surroundings that reaffirm the idea that white solidarity is the way to organize your world, even while doing antiracist work, then how are you not going to believe that a constructed all-white world isn't you at your most functioning? How isn't that going to feel natural and right? Stark, yes. Ironic, yes.

Not long after this conversation, a white male friend attends a diversity workshop. He sends me crazy emoji faces during the faculty and staff workshop. I call as soon as he indicates the workshop is over. The session was run by two white women. Only one black faculty member was in the group. All participants were given examples of a classroom situation that seems to clearly involve racism.

The scenario states: "While teaching a section on African Art you display the following image and ask students what they think of the image. A student states that the image 'looks like a monkey.' Some students in the class laugh at the response and some black students look upset."

The people in the workshop say the comparison between a black person and a monkey is a joke. Jokes can be used to own and not to

Text *Comparing a black person to a monkey is one of the oldest and most expedient forms of racism . . .*

Notes and Sources The philosopher Charles Mills and sociologist Wulf Hund edited a volume on "simianization," which collects essays on dehumanization as a form of racism with particular attention to the comparison to apes. It offers both a review of contemporary cases of this form of racism and a history. The volume, given its publication date, does not include former BBC broadcaster Danny Baker's tweet, which contained the image below referencing the birth of the royal mixed-race baby in 2019.

own a moment, a feeling, or a racist feeling. I'm kidding. Lighten up. Jokes allow one to run from and own a thing simultaneously.

No one mentions Pamela Ramsey Taylor, who commented on Facebook that "it will be so refreshing to have a classy, beautiful, dignified First Lady back in the White House. I'm tired of seeing a [*sic*] Ape in heels."

Comparing a black person to a monkey is one of the oldest and most expedient forms of racism in the unwritten manual of white supremacy. *Saturday Night Live* cast member Leslie Jones felt compelled to tweet: "OK I have been called Apes, sent pics of their asses, even got a pic with semen on my face. I'm trying to figure out what human means. I'm out."

Was it a white person who made the comparison in the scenario? My emphasis is on "white" and not on "person." The individual referenced is less important than the use of the word "monkey," which attempts to erase the personhood of the one it attaches to. Don't "monkey this up," Florida governor Ron DeSantis said during his 2018 gubernatorial race, and we all understood the statement historically meant don't vote for the black candidate even as DeSantis denied it.

Text *Theorist Benjamin Eleanor Adam observes that Google searches for the term "evolution" result in portrayals of the height of evolution as the body of a white male . . .*

Notes and Sources In her book *Rethinking Evolution in the Museum: Envisioning African Origins*, scholar Monique Scott describes these linear illustrations of evolution, from nineteenth-century Darwinian discourses to F. Clark Howell's 1965 Time-Life book *Early Man*, the first representation of men marching single file. Scott writes, "Images from the earliest evolutionary books, newspapers, and exhibitions illustrate that from the earliest incarnation of human evolution, the concept has been accompanied by such visual progress narratives . . . the 'march of progress' image."

Also see the interview "James Baldwin Discusses the Problem of Being White in America" (1985): "When Americans say change in the generality, they really mean progress. And when they say progress, they really mean—and they don't know they mean this—they really mean how quickly and to what extent and how profoundly a black person becomes white. They take themselves quite helplessly as the only possible model of what they call change."

Theorist Benjamin Eleanor Adam observes that Google searches for the term "evolution" result in portrayals of the height of evolution as the body of a white male, thereby "relating whiteness and humanity, an association that has its roots in racial science and ethical justifications of colonialism, slavery, and genocide. . . . By presenting whites as the quintessential humans who possess the bodies and behaviors taken to be deeply meaningful human traits, whites justified, and continue to justify, white supremacy." Hence the use of the word "monkey" in relationship to black people places white men in the primary position on the evolutionary line, an idiocy addressed by James Baldwin in an interview entitled "James Baldwin Discusses the Problem of Being White in America": "Whites sought to civilize black people before civilizing themselves."

If the structure that structures the scenario is itself racist, are the questions trick questions?

In the diversity workshop, no one asks why the scenario leaves out the race of the student who states that the image of the black figure "looks like a monkey." That might be helpful. White? Asian? Latinx? I extrapolate that the one who made the statement isn't black since the black students are marked by their race: "Some Black students look upset." Is it beyond conceivable that white students could also be upset by this, or Asian students or Latinx students or black Asian students or black Latinx or indigenous or . . . ? Since there exists no scenario where white students are upset by the statement, are we to understand any distress they would feel to be insincere, passing, and not actionable?

As reported by my friend, the white faculty and staff in the room insist on giving the "joking student" (is he/she/they white?) the benefit of the doubt. The lone black male faculty member in the

Text *If white people don't see their whiteness, how can they speak to it? Was the student white? Who wrote the scenario? Does diversity not include any training to see ourselves . . . ?*

Notes and Sources See "Try and Make Me! Why Corporate Diversity Training Fails," published by the American Sociological Association in 2007, for a history of diversity training, starting in 1961 with John F. Kennedy's executive order making it a requirement for federal contractors to take "affirmative action" against discrimination. By 2005, diversity training was offered by 65 percent of large firms and companies.

room offers up the thought that maybe the student didn't mean anything by it. He, too, is willing to give the student (is he/she/they white?) the benefit of the doubt.

My white friend waited to see what the white women leading the workshop would say. They said nothing. The facilitators moved on after everyone who wished to respond responded, despite the fact that white women in management are usually the ones calling for diversity training. Only then did my friend interrupt to point out that while it might be a joke, it's still a racist joke. If you all are hearing it as an innocent comment, what's innocent about it? he asked. The black faculty member changed his alliances to support my white friend. Yes, that's right, he added. Only then did the others suggest that the student (is he/she/they white?) be taken aside and spoken to. I wondered about the phrase "taken aside."

The taking aside lends privacy to the act, putting the student's statement outside of the room, and fails to take into account the public distress the student (is he/she/they white?) occasioned.

At the periphery of my friend's descriptions of the afternoon diversity training session there remains a question: If white people don't see their whiteness, how can they speak to it? Was the student white? Who wrote the scenario? Does diversity not include any training to see ourselves or is it simply about addressing black grievance?

After hanging up the phone, I walked to my front door and opened it. The lawn was covered by fallen leaves. For all its apparent beauty, the dead leaves were rotting. Staring into the leaves, I remembered that weeks before a white woman said to me,

from James Baldwin's *The White Man's Guilt*

I have often wondered, and it is not a pleasant wonder,
just what white Americans talk about with one another.

I wonder this because they do not,
after all, seem to find very much to say to *me*,
and I concluded long ago that they found the color

of my skin inhibitory. This color
seems to operate as a most disagreeable mirror,
and a great deal of one's energy is expended

in reassuring white Americans
that they do not see what they see. This is utterly
futile, of course, since they *do* see what they see.

And what they see is an appallingly oppressive
and bloody history, known all over the world.
What they see is a disastrous, continuing, present

condition which menaces them, and for which
they bear an inescapable responsibility.

But since, in the main, they seem to lack the energy
to change this condition,
they would rather not be reminded of it.

Does this mean that in their conversations
with one another, they merely make reassuring sounds?

It scarcely seems possible, and yet, on the other hand,
it seems all too likely.

"I've been doing antiracist work since the eighties. I'm here to tell you it makes no difference." In the moment I laughed with my full face. My laughter was so embodied she started to laugh as well. What were we laughing about? The air was crisp. I closed the door and returned to my desk, where I dawdled by lineating ● a statement from a Baldwin interview.

lemonade

Text *I tell her rather dramatically that the Internet of health statistics claimed I should be dead . . .*

Notes and Sources See the CDC report *Breast Cancer Rates among Black Women and White Women*:

"Black women and white women get breast cancer at about the same rate, but black women die from breast cancer at a higher rate than white women.

"Compared with white women, black women had lower rates of getting breast cancer (*incidence rates*) and higher rates of dying from breast cancer (*death rates*) between 1999 and 2013. During this period, breast cancer incidence went down among white women, and went up slightly among black women. Now, breast cancer incidence is about the same for women of both races.

"Deaths from breast cancer are going down among both black and white women, especially among younger black women. But breast cancer death rates are 40% higher among black women than white women."

I too remember
being shook

The blond marriage counselor is clearly a brunette. I wonder if the yellowing of her hair is intended to take her a step closer to desirability outside of the office or relatability within it? Where do I fit in? None of these thoughts do I share as my husband and I sit across from her in the office; instead I tell her rather dramatically that the Internet of health statistics claimed I should be dead, but it was the twenty-first century, and after a year of being made nauseated by toxic chemotherapy drugs and radiation, I now feel better.

The threat of imminent death had built a mansion in my mind where before there existed only a motel for passing fears. In obedience to my new reality, I lived in three-month intervals between blood work. Would there be elevated levels of protein cells indicating my cancer's return? The cells stayed still, and then, one day as we drove to the hospital, as if I were Denzel Washington's character in the film adaptation of the August Wilson play *Fences*, I sat in a speeding car, and because metaphors can also be realities, speedily informed my husband that, in my remaining time, though always the time remains unknown, I needed to find a partner who would make me laugh. It was a humorless moment and so proved my point. This is how we'd ended up in this marriage counselor's office after twenty years of a high-functioning marriage full of collaborations and films and parenting and dog walking and sharing novels and hosting dinner parties.

Both my husband and I in our decades together spent much of our time making art addressing the racist treatment of American citizens. We tracked police shootings of unarmed black people; we tracked legislators and judges who were committed to mass incarceration; we shared articles about black children being treated worse than animals by law enforcement; we both cried shamelessly

when a black girl was thrown across the classroom by a white male school resource officer and when a black girl at a pool party was slammed to the ground in McKinney, Texas, by a white policeman. Year in and year out we listened and exchanged looks as white people said egregiously racist things in our presence. We attempted to make sense of it all in coherent narratives and images. We fought about esoteric issues like point of view and mundane ones like money. Over the years, we walked miles inside museums and sat hours inside theaters considering how to do what we do better. We helped each other in our endeavors and were pleased by each other's achievements. My husband calmed me down when confronted by inequity and I calmed him down when confronted by bureaucracy. And so the years passed.

Though we wouldn't stop, this once I suggested we redirect the drive that was our life. My husband told the counselor I had communicated deeply painful things over the past months, the worst of which was when I'd told him he should go forward with confidence into divorce-freedom, because as a tall, blue-eyed, middle-aged white man in reasonably good shape, he would have no trouble replacing me, a black woman, in America.

This was a hurtful thing to say, it seemed to the counselor, not because it was untrue, but because my husband felt hurt by it. This ability to separate fact from affect is what one learns in therapy.

When I met my husband at thirty, he was serious-minded and fully aware of what racism made possible. I came to know him through his work first: images of African American children whose life circumstances no one deserved. His understanding of racial politics and the justice system in the United States was more various and clear-eyed than my own. I didn't have to convince him, or

show him, or explain anything about how white antiblack racism worked. He heard the slights in real time. It was a relief. He was the relief. It was with him I entered my first prisons to visit over-sentenced youth. He made a difference in the lives he encountered without having economic privilege or legal access. He visited as a friend. From him I learned what it meant to simply show up and take a picture of what you saw.

Do you not value yourself? The counselor asks this as if she had never seen how black women are treated in the world. Of course I do, I say slowly to give myself time to figure out her line of reason. I am not talking about myself. I can't support, marry, or integrate myself. This I say to give her time to consider what she will say next. Don't you understand how much your husband values you? is her next question. Okay, I say. But isn't my husband, whoever else he is, also white America?

It's an obvious no; but even the obvious is inside history, so, yes too. I wonder if the question she should be asking is if a carefree love can come out of a shared interest in white rage and white violence against black people inside a democratic structure that constructs, sponsors, and supports this behavior. I can't be an expert in my own subjugation and it's certainly not where I find pleasure. We could talk about that perhaps. Then I think maybe bringing up my husband's whiteness was a way of giving him back whatever he might lose if I died or departed. Perhaps it was a way to say, you win. You will win. Cancer is me losing and even if I find the joke in it all it is still me losing. You won. Can't you see that? But no one wins when it's cancer or time they're bargaining with.

Had the counselor asked me what I felt was the most hurtful thing I'd said to my husband, I wouldn't say what he said since my

statement just seemed like a truth we'd all seen play itself out in other marriages around us. But as I scan my memory, it was in fact the only thing I'd said that pointed directly to his whiteness. Considering the fact that I know white people don't like to be called white, I wonder if I said it to hurt my husband, since so many words in those months seemed like they were tossed out as fighting words. Though admittedly at the time I was the least equipped person to judge my own subtext, however much I looked at it, my claim continued to feel like the truth of the matter.

Centered in hurt and history, Beyoncé's *Lemonade* addresses infidelity, four hundred years of racism and its effects on devastated black families, none of which were wholly our issues but I still find it consoling. Perhaps it's because the "visual album" also addresses black love, or is it just love? Beyoncé zoomed us out in order to see how all of history was against the success of her marriage and she isn't wrong. My own interracial marriage also existed inside a racist America whose ways make life more difficult. Many times driving in New York City and New Jersey (we lived in the South only one year), we were pulled over by police and asked how we knew each other; there are all the places my husband walks into while I'm stopped at the door; and there are the white women who understood our relationship to be anything but a marriage as they step between us to flirt. We laughed about these moments in real time, but it was not this kind of laughter I was after.

Our laughter came out of moments when the world, its structures, did all the talking. This laughter was reactive and served as a nod to idiocy and violence. It was a laughter that understood, even as we felt the blows landing. It was a laughter of "what can

you do?" and "oh my God." We laughed at what we saw, what we knew, what we experienced, and hardly did we speak beyond it. Our lives, our marriage, our collaborations are built in this world.

Was there a possibility of a love and a laughter that lived outside the structure that brought us together? Who could I tell that though I would never walk away from my life, sometimes I have wanted to? *There is a pain—so utter—It swallows substance up—*Who could I tell and have the telling not be a threat or an expressed desire to be punished? *So memory can step around—across—upon it—*Who could I tell where the telling itself would be a space to inhabit and perhaps, maybe, even joke about one stormy night? Now this would be a good day to leave, the imagined one would say. This would be a love that is not defended, that had a deadpan humor about tomorrows. What would that feel like in any America?

In this America we had yet to achieve the laughter that came up out of our own conversations, our own crazy logic, our own wishful wants, that finds its place in reality though it is not any reality you can have without knowing a person really or at least trying to comprehend the individual pathways we each build so we can hold ourselves together. The poet Erica Hunt describes love as "a close reading" that "help[s] me invent myself more—in the future." It's the most workable definition I've found to date.

People feel hurt when you point out the reality that forms experience because the reality is not their emotional experience, the counselor reminded us that day. The structures that inform our lives are the predetermined architecture we live in or against. But I am beginning to know that feelings can change structures. If many white men can have much of what they want, including

81

While [we] do remain together there must be a position of superior and inferior, and I, as much as any other man, am in favor of having the superior position assigned to the white race. I say upon this occasion I do not perceive that because the white man is to have the superior position the negro should be denied everything. I do not understand that because I do not want a negro woman for a slave I must necessarily want her for a wife.

Abraham Lincoln

potential anonymous women of any age they have yet to meet, in a society set up to support them with images of officers and gentlemen and Don Drapers, that does not mean, the counselor implied, my husband wouldn't be devastated by my absence.

And if the black woman is the most disrespected, unprotected, and neglected person in America, as Malcolm X told us before he was assassinated, and as Beyoncé reminded us in her "visual album" *Lemonade*, that didn't mean I would perish if my life lacked humor, as it did while I was dying. There is something to be said for staying alongside in our sobering reality. Some realities aren't funny. They are made up of truths more vital than laughable no matter how much or how little time you have.

outstretched

We must travel through a cloudy veil to arrive at a human object. Whiteness is in the way of seeing. We can barely hold on to what's being approached. I think about what it means to soften an image, as in its memory, as in its future memory. The filter covers our pupils and acts as a kind of cataract even as our black circular openings open to the light. Vision is blurred and all statements are projections, guesses, educated and not. The more one looks, the more the eyes attempt to focus, to lock down a narrative. It's a strain to formulate a declarative sentence. But now a woman appears as if an apparition took hold. There is a black woman at the center of things who lives amidst the whiteness. The photograph's title, *Woman with Arms Outstretched*, asks us to look closely at what she is doing. The language of the title, "outstretched," seems an overstatement, an interesting one—optimistic in its reach for the future, a time ahead of her. What is she evidence of? Do time's constraints turn out to be human constraints? Once I confused the passage of time with change. It was a careless use of language's unfreedoms. The rhetoric of whiteness spawned brutal confusion. Even now, years later, years away, in the world of the image, one waits. The woman's arms seem slightly activated at her sides. Their movement is caught by the image. Does the photograph reflect the moment before the action realized by the title's claim? What can one know from either the photographed moment or its title? I am beginning to wonder if outstretched is a way to call forward a yearning. Her arms open to arrival. What is it she sees coming? Longing floods the whiteness. The photograph captures an urban American landscape containing a black woman, "edited out of our seeing," as the photographer Paul Graham describes her. The photograph belongs to his series *American Night*. Maybe the yearning I attach to the image originates with the white photographer. Perhaps the white haze is his own attempt to see what the American landscape holds just out of his sight, for

Text *A necropastoral. This term is not in the dictionary. Where did I first hear it? It too does not exist and yet it was said and is now being repeated.*

Fact Check Yes, it's not in the dictionary but defined by Joyelle McSweeney below.

Notes and Sources "What Is the Necropastoral?" by Joyelle McSweeney: "I first wrote about the Necropastoral in January of 2011. The Necropastoral is a political-aesthetic zone in which the fact of mankind's depredations cannot be separated from an experience of 'nature' which is poisoned, mutated, aberrant, spectacular, full of ill effects and affects. The Necropastoral is a non-rational zone, anachronistic, it often looks backwards and does not subscribe to Cartesian coordinates or Enlightenment notions of rationality and linearity, cause and effect. It does not subscribe to humanism but is interested in non-human modalities, like those of bugs, viruses, weeds and mold."

white men, for white people. All people? Graham says you have to choose to overcome your own blindness as he slows down the process of seeing by overexposing the image. He wishes to communicate the difficulty of knowing through seeing. Is the woman in the scene walking her dog? The dog is a bag. I can make out the handles. She has placed it on the ground to free up her hands. She's prepared to wait. Once she stops being the object of the photographer's gaze, she could do something else. Or, she is forever outdoors in the imaginary of our democracy, locked forever on the street confirming the white photographer's vision of blackness. Or, in the moment after the shutter closes, does the bus arrive? The grass on which she stands is not a destination. It is not nature. It is a patch of dry grass, a median strip, between infrastructures, between lanes of traffic, between nowhere and here, between him and her, between him and me, between me and you. It's a racialized enclosure. A necropastoral. This term is ● not in the dictionary. Where did I first hear it? It too does not exist and yet it was said and is now being repeated. I was born. In a slave narrative that means nothing. Meaningless. I was born and in the midst of this photograph I am now being repeated so that the photographer can see what whiteness has erased and is erasing and will erase because white life enacts the problem of erasure. There are other words too: hoses, dogs, genocide, incarceration, assassination, wall, immigration, Can I help you? Why are you here? Do you live here? Can I see your ID? Is this your house? Is she your wife? Inside the shape of the woman is there a woman? As I am being human am I a human being? Arms outstreched? My ass. My stance as life stretches out into seconds, minutes, days, weeks, months, years, decades. Once it was 1619. The month was August. I sat staring into an image unfolding. Life. A film of whiteness. That's when the alarm in my house went off. I followed the sound to the Atlantic.

daughter

Because I want the world for my daughter, and I do mean the world, I have my most corrupt thought of the year. It's time for the fall parent-teacher meetings at her predominantly white high school, and I think, if her white father goes on his own, her teachers' unconscious racial bias won't be triggered by me to land on her. Oh God. Oh God. Oh God.

Eleven people have just been shot in a synagogue by a white terrorist. "You will not replace us, Jews will not replace us" was the chant that filled the streets in Charlottesville two summers before. "Very fine people on both sides" was how the nationalist-identified president saw it. Two black people have been shot in Kroger's after a white nationalist can't get inside a black church. Black church after black church is being burned down, this after nine people were gunned down in Bible study at Emanuel African Methodist Episcopal Church by a white supremacist described as having "sad eyes," pipe bombs have been mailed by a domestic terrorist to the offices of major media and Democratic political figures, and, and, and. After a flurry of hate mail, an alarm system has just been installed at my home that both reassures me and makes me feel like I live in a fort inside a civil war. A friend who has dropped by just as the mailperson arrives tells me not to open the packages inside the house. Because I want this world for my daughter?

Another white friend tells me she has to defend me all the time to her white friends who think I'm a radical. Why? For calling white people white? For not wanting unarmed black people to be gunned down in our streets or black girls to be flung across classrooms and thrown to the ground by officers? (Most, so far, by white men in the documented cases.) What does that even mean? I ask her. Don't defend me. Not for being human. Not for wanting others to be able to just live their lives. Not for wanting us to simply be able to live.

Text *As we sit across from her white teachers, I smile and nod but really only want to ask them if they actively think about their unconscious inevitable racism and implicit bias, which is unavoidable given our world, the very world I want for my daughter.*

Notes and Sources In "The Power of Teacher Expectations: How Racial Bias Hinders Student Attainment," Seth Gershenson and Nicholas Papageorge used the Education Longitudinal Study of 2002 (which "followed a cohort of 10th-grade students for a decade" and included a survey of teacher expectations about their students) to find that "white teachers, who comprise the vast majority of American educators, have far lower expectations for black students than they do for similarly situated white students. This evidence suggests that to raise student attainment, particularly among students of color, elevating teacher expectations, eliminating racial bias, and hiring a more diverse teaching force are worthy goals." See also the same authors in the *Economics of Education Review* article "Who Believes in Me? The Effect of Student-Teacher Demographic Match on Teacher Expectations," by Seth Gershenson, Stephen B. Holt, and Nicholas W. Papageorge.

The desire to stay home from the parent-teacher conference makes a kind of sense even as the thought unsettles me, begins me stumbling around in my head, but either way, it couldn't prevent me from going to meet my daughter's teachers. As we step into the gymnasium at the school, my white husband mentions he doesn't see any teachers of color. Since I haven't shared my version of this thought with him, his anxiety might or might not have anything to do with me.

"ANYONE TELLING ANYTHING IS TELLING THAT THING," states the Eve Fowler print hanging in our home. It's there as a reminder. What thing is my husband telling? If he stayed with his articulated thought long enough, would he end up in the same fucked-up place with me staying at home so I don't trigger the white teachers' racial bias? Would he wish me to leave because I am underrepresented? Is he feeling overrepresented? What is that feeling? Is he flooded by his own whiteness? Or is he simply in solution mode? Whatever the case, he's also having feelings. Is he feeling anxious about the world or this particular place? Both?

Oh God. We count only two black teachers. Our daughter is in neither of their classes. We know our daughter loves her classes and speaks highly of her teachers. OK. OK. As we sit across from her white teachers, I smile and nod but really only want to ask them if they actively think about their unconscious inevitable racism and implicit bias, which is unavoidable given our world, the very world I want for my daughter. It's a mouthful. I could choke on it.

Each of her teachers wishes to know if we have any questions. Only one question lives and breathes between us. Only one question

And what that meant was that generations of young African-American children were pushed to achieve this mission [of integration]. And we sent them into places that were unsafe, where they were humiliated, and their egos were decimated in structures—as Toni Morrison said, "Out there, they don't love our children." And these generations of African-American children have felt abandoned, and there's a chasm that has grown up between younger and older African Americans, based on this sense of younger people, of having felt that they were abandoned. And they don't understand, why did we send them, young children, into places like that without any protection?

Ruby Sales

pulls at me like a child wanting my attention. Reassure me. Do it. Come on. Do it. Knowing that the DNA of whiteness includes defending itself from my knowledge of our shared history to the point of becoming ahistorical and framing everything economically or universally as if that erases racism, what would, what could they say? *I know I am white and your daughter is of mixed race and you are black.* If we started there, then what? *I know and sometimes I think . . .* What do you think? More importantly, what do you think when you are not thinking?

Looking around, I wonder about all the white parents surrounding me. Are any of them anxious that these white teachers are overrepresenting the race of their child and therefore affirming white dominance and white hierarchical thinking? Are any concerned that these white teachers, with their overwhelming representation of whiteness, are confirming the racist structures we are all subject to? What is my aim here?

I don't know if my daughter is negotiating the same moments I did as a high school student. How could she? She is not me. For all that I have said, for all that she has read, how is it going for her in real time? Why haven't I warmed up to the systemic structures affirming my own nonworth? What would I need to see? What would I need to feel in order to trust that my daughter will be given the space she needs to just be as she sits in their classrooms?

What would it take for me to feel somewhat at ease? A group of white parents approaching me and my husband to express anxiety about the lack of diversity among the faculty? A group of faculty approaching us to say we know what this looks like? Maybe

I truly want to believe I don't know the answers since I don't know the answers. Maybe I want to believe somewhere in this vast gymnasium there is a crack—a crack in my own imaginative possibilities. I want the world for my daughter.

My own high school and college days were peppered with teachers who went out of their way to help me. All of them were white in the private and Catholic schools I attended. It just takes one is the anecdotal logic or the circumstantial luck. But for every teacher I remember who was supportive, I can remember two or three who were socialized not to see me. As a teenager I didn't take their behavior personally. They were a thing to watch. Even back then, regarding the ones who ignored my hand in the air and for whom I disappeared, I passively understood their disregard or indifference as "white people stuff," instinctive rather than responsive.

I ask a white friend with three mixed-race children, now grown, if she'd worried about their treatment at school. She says she really only worried if the teacher would "get" her child. "Does the teacher understand my particular child is what I thought about," she explained. For high school she'd attended Miss Porter's School for girls, and back then she hadn't thought about any teacher's relationship to their whiteness. With her own children, though they are black-identified, she didn't worry about their schools' predominantly white staff and student body. Thinking back, she remembers being asked by a teacher, how old were her kids when she adopted them? The thought of a black father did not enter the white teacher's imagination. Her son remembers another teacher who asked his mom, how can this be your son if he doesn't have your blond hair? I guess I was naive, she adds as an afterthought.

Text *... white parents who are now living in the gentrified district resisted the integration of the public middle schools that are now predominantly white.*

Notes and Sources According to a 2016 study by the Furman Center that tracks the gentrification of New York City neighborhoods, in the Harlem section of District 3 and adjoining areas, Hamilton Heights, Manhattanville, and West Harlem, the white population increased by 55 percent, along with the Asian and Hispanic populations. The black population dropped by 41 percent.

Michael W. Kraus, Julian M. Rucker, and Jennifer A. Richards, "Americans misperceive racial economic equality" (PNAS: Proceedings of the National Academy of Sciences of the United States of America): "The results of the present studies suggest that Americans largely misperceive race-based economic equality. Indeed, our results suggest a systematic tendency to perceive greater progress toward racial economic equality than has actually been achieved, largely driven by overestimates of current levels of equality. Although this tendency to overestimate current racial economic equality was observed among both White and Black Americans, there was also a significant status divide in the magnitude of these misperceptions: high-income White Americans' overestimates of current racial economic equality were larger than those generated by low-income White Americans and by Black Americans across the income distribution. Further, the present results suggest that the tendency to overestimate racial equality is likely shaped by both motivational and structural factors that lead people to deny and/or remain unaware of the ways in which race continues to shape economic outcomes in contemporary society."

Text *The plan would mean children with lower test scores (hear: race-based economic inequality) would have a chance to attend a school with better resources.*

Notes and Sources
Chalkbeat: "Another Integration Plan for Upper West Side Middle Schools Is Met with Some Support, but Also Familiar Concerns," by Christina Veiga: "Though diversity has generally been shown to benefit students, . . . [a parent at P.S. 84] pointed to studies that showed negative effects when students were mixed by ability levels. 'The research suggests it won't work and in fact may backfire,' he said. 'I think mandating academic diversity and taking a one size fits all approach is a disservice.'"

This idea of a shared anxiety with other white parents regarding the lack of diversity at my daughter's school seems an idle thought. I am trying it on though I know many of my white friends are only now grappling with what comes along with their whiteness in the face of a nationalist presidency, the least of which is what it means to have been brought up by white people who were brought up by white people who were brought up by white people who were brought up by slave owners, or not. This is why no one should have been surprised by the District 3 public school debate on the Upper West Side and in South Harlem, where "woke" white parents who are now living in the gentrified district resisted the integration of the public middle schools that are now predominantly white. Many white parents were outraged at the thought of making 25 percent of school seats open to children scoring below standards on proficiency tests who qualified for free and reduced-cost lunch, a move that would make the student body more diverse. Their anxiety that their child might no longer have a seat in the school manifested in incredulous rage that was shared with the world by the school principal defending integration. His surprise at their behavior surprises me. What population did he think he was serving?

The plan would mean children with lower test scores (hear: race-based economic inequality) would have a chance to attend a school with better resources. As reported, one white parent argued that to bring less prepared students into the local public school would create "impostor syndrome" for those children. Did he believe they would be pretending to be white or pretending to be educated? "Whether it's based on academics, on race, on economics—segregation is bad for kids," one principal argued. "When we're a family, we try to look out for the best interest of all kids, not just the ones in our households." Another white parent felt, as reported by the *New York Post*, "There are some

Text *The inability of white people to see children other than white children as children is a reality that frankly leaves one hopeless about a change in attitudes regarding the perceived humanity of black people.*

Notes and Sources Juliet Hooker, "Black Protest / White Grievance: On the Problem of White Political Imagination Not Shaped by Loss" (*The South Atlantic Quarterly*): "The political imagination of white citizens has been shaped not by the experience of loss but rather by different forms of white supremacy and . . . this results in a distorted form of racial political math that sees black gains as white losses, and not simply losses but defeats. As a result, in moments when white privilege is in crisis because white dominance is threatened, many white citizens not only are unable or unwilling to recognize black suffering; they mobilize a sense of white victimhood in response."

Text *We are a sad lot churning inside the repetitions and insistences of the "afterlife of slavery."*

Notes and Sources Saidiya Hartman, *Lose Your Mother: A Journey along the Atlantic Slave Route*: "If slavery persists as an issue in the political life of black America, it is not because of an antiquarian obsession with bygone days or the burden of a too-long memory, but because black lives are still imperiled and devalued by a racial calculus and a political arithmetic that were entrenched centuries ago. This is the afterlife of slavery—skewed life chances, limited access to health and education, premature death, incarceration, and impoverishment. I, too, am the afterlife of slavery."

really good middle schools in New York City and it shouldn't just be rich kids who get to go to them. . . . School integration is scary. Even when it's the right answer, it's scary." Does he mean proximity to nonwhites is a threat?

The inability of white people to see children other than white children as children is a reality that frankly leaves one hopeless about a change in attitudes regarding the perceived humanity of black people. The phrase "they are just kids" exists with the unspoken "except when they are black." The full thought lives beneath the civility of more whites than can be imagined and many "exceptional" people of color whose economics bring them closer to their identification with white dominance and antiblack racism. There also exist blacks who are embarrassed by black and brown poverty because they see life through the judging lenses of white discrimination and understand their own exceptionalism as tenuous inasmuch as its optics are stained by a disadvantaged black population at large. We are a sad lot churning inside the repetitions and insistences of the "afterlife of slavery."

In addition, a bill that would have replaced the standardized SHSAT test and given the top children from all the city's middle schools access to free magnet high schools never made it to the floor of the New York Senate. Eliza Shapiro and Vivian Wang reported that "some Asian families argued that the mayor's plan discriminated against the low-income Asian students who are now a majority at the schools." For example, Shapiro and Wang pointed out that of the 895 seats available at Stuyvesant High School in 2019, only 7 went to black students. Low-income black and Hispanic students are dispensable in conversations regarding segregation in both middle schools and high schools apparently. We knew the position of many white parents in policies that would integrate

Text *Someone white who is not wholly identified with whiteness, even as he is still capable of being surprised by its Jim Crow ways.*

Fact Check Yes, education and Jim Crow connection.

Notes and Sources Frederick Douglass to Unknown (transcribed):

My dear sir:

Washington, D.C., November 23, 1887

Pardon delay—answer to your letter made careful enquiry necessary. From all I can learn colored Lawyers are admitted to practice in Southern Courts, and I am very glad to admit the fact—for it implies a wonderful revolution in the public sentiment of the Southern States. I have not yet learned what are the inequalities between the races as to school privileges at the south—In some of the states the time allotted to colored schools is less than that allowed to whites. And I have heard and believe that in none of the states are the teachers of colored Schools as well paid as the teachers of White Schools. My own observation has been that white teachers of Colored schools in the southern states, show but little interest in their pupils. This is not strange, since they have been selected as teachers more because of their necessities, than from any interests they have shown in the progress and elevation of the colored race. [*struck*: bu] I say this not of all, but of those in Virginia for instance who have come under my observation.

In Kentucky I believe so far as the law is concerned equal advantages are extended to colored children for Education, and the Same may be true of other states. I think the Bureau of Education will give you all the information you may require on this branch of the subject of your enquiries, our wrongs are not so much now in written laws which all may see—but the hidden practices of a people who have not yet abandoned the idea of Mastery and dominion over their fellow man.

With great Respect Yours truly

Fredk Douglass
Cedar Hill Anacostia D.C. Nov: 23. 1887

black and brown children, but now some Asian parents are taking on the racially coded rhetoric and positions usually heard from some whites.

The Upper West Side school principal's vigilance in the District 3 debate is perhaps the element of surprise that my husband and I are seeking in the world of our child. Someone white who is not wholly identified with whiteness, even as he is still capable of being surprised by its Jim Crow ways.

What is it we want for our daughter? Perhaps it's the ability to negotiate the world with an empathic imagination. The thing that brought both my husband and me to the gymnasium is the knowledge that though the deep-seated racist systems are re-affirmed and the evidence is there for us to see, I still want the world for my daughter that is more than this world, a world that has our daughter already in it.

notes on the state of whiteness

NOTES on the ftate of VIRGINIA;

written in the year 1781, fomewhat corrected and enlarged in the winter of 1782, for the ufe of a Foreigner of diftinction, in anfwer to certain queries propofed by him refpecting

MDCCLXXXII.

To change the rules of descent, so as that the lands of any person dying intestate shall be divisible equally among all his children or other representatives in equal degree.

To make slaves distributable among the next of kin, as other moveables.

To emancipate all slaves born after pasfing the act. The bill reported by the revifors does not itfelf contain this propofition; but an amendment containing it was prepared, to be offered to the legiflature whenever the bill fhould be taken up,

It will probably be asked, Why not retain and incorporate the blacks into the state, and thus save the expence of supplying, by importation of white settlers, the vacancies they will leave? Deep rooted prejudices entertained by the whites; ten thousand recollections, by the blacks, of the injuries they have sustained; new provocations; the real distinctions which nature has made; and many other circumstances, will divide us into parties, and produce convulsions which will probably never end but in the extermination of the one or the other race.--- The first difference which strikes us is that of colour. Whether the black of the negro resides in the reticular membrane between the skin and scarf skin, or in the scarf skin itself;

whether it proceeds from the colour of the blood, the colour of the bile, or from that of some other secretion, the difference is fixed in nature, and is as real as if its seat and cause were better known to us. And is this difference of no importance? Is it not the foundation of a greater or less share of beauty in the two races? Are not the fine mixtures of red and white, the expressions of every passion by greater or less suffusions of colour in the one, preferable to that eternal monotony, which reigns in the countenances, that immoveable veil of black, which covers all the emotions of the other race? Add to these, flowing hair, a more elegant symmetry of form, their own judgment in favour of the whites, declared by their preference of them as uniformly as is the preference of the Oran-ootan for the black women over those of his own species. The circumstance of superior beauty, is thought worthy attention in the propagation of our horses, dogs and other domestic animals; why not in that of man? Besides those of colour, figure, and hair, there are other physical distinctions proving a difference of race. They have less hair on the face and body. They secrete

Perhaps too a difference of ſtructure in the pulmonary apparatus, which a late ingenious *experimentaliſt has diſcovered to be the principal regulator of animal heat, may have diſabled them from extricating, in the act of inſpiration

They ſeem to require leſs ſleep.

They are at leaſt as brave

---

* Crawford.

Their griefs are transient.

  In general, their existence appears to participate more of sensation than reflection. To this must be ascribed their disposition to sleep when abstracted from their diversions, and unemployed in labour. An animal whose body is at rest, and who does not reflect, must be disposed to sleep of course.

  it appears to me that in memory they are equal to the whites; in reason much inferior.

  It would be unfair to follow them to Africa for this investigation. We will consider them here, on the same stage with the whites

Many millions of them have been brought to, and born in America.

many have been so situated that they might have availed themselves of the conversation of their masters

Some have been liberally educated

They will crayon out an animal, a plant, or a country, so as to prove the existence of a germ in their minds which only wants cultivation.

But never
yet could I find that a black had uttered a
thought above the level of plain narration;
never fee even an elementary trait of paint-
ing or fculpture. In mufic they are more
generally gifted than the whites with accu-
rate ears for tune and time

Mifery is often the parent of
the moft affecting touches in poetry.——
Among the blacks is mifery enough, God
knows, but no poetry.

it could not produce
a poet.

tiki torches

TIKI Brand Products
56 mins · 🌐

TIKI Brand is not associated in any way with the
events that took place in Charlottesville and are
deeply saddened and disappointed. We do not
support their message or the use of our products in
this way. Our products are designed to enhance
backyard gatherings and to help family and friends
connect with each other at home in their yard.

6 Shares

 LIKE　　　 COMMENT　　　 SHARE

 18

A year after James Alex Fields Jr. intentionally drove into a group of people protesting a Nazi march and killed Heather Heyer in Charlottesville, Virginia, I mention to a white male friend that though there was a cross burning the fall before we arrived at college in 1981, back then I did not realize how many white supremacist terrorist acts were essentially about me. My presence, even as I was unknown and invisible to whoever set it ablaze that year, was being marked as an American target. It's been almost forty years and my friend, sitting across from me at his dining room table, says he had no idea our alma mater was the site of a cross burning. No one had mentioned it.

This white man and I have seen each other infrequently but consistently over the years. He attends my events, which I take as support of our friendship and my endeavors. I am fond of both him and his wife, and though I've never visited him in particular, meeting up is always a bonus when I find myself in the Twin Cities. We have squeezed in a dinner here and there, narrated the lives of our children, and checked in with each other about mutual friends. The years pass, and we maintain the same level of comfort and familiarity. I liked him at eighteen and I like him in my middle ages, but I wonder if it's an overstatement to think of the memory of the cross burning as a fundamental difference or a deficiency of something between us.

I say, I'm pretty sure it happened.

We both pull out our phones.

Wow, he says, having located the event in the memory bank of his search engine.

Text *Could our closeness in college be attributed in part to an understanding of what remains possible given our history?*

Notes and Sources The photograph is of the 1925 Klan march in Washington. The *Washington Post* offered two retrospectives in 1982 and 2018. The Klan apparently attempted to reproduce the march a number of times, including in 1982. A few details about the original march from the 1982 retrospective: "According to The Post articles, the largest state delegations came not from the South but from New Jersey and Pennsylvania. Acting Police Supt. Charles A. Evans . . . estimated the crowd at between 30,000 and 35,000." (Higher estimates noted; see the *Atlantic* article cited below.) "The Klansmen came by more than 18 special trains. . . . The rhetoric of the parade, according to the pictures and news accounts of the time, was focused primarily not on race but on 'Americanism' and the cultural fears of a people who saw themselves imperiled by immigration. . . . Anti-Catholic sentiment was particularly high."

See also Joshua Rothman, "When Bigotry Paraded through the Streets," the *Atlantic*: "On August 8, 1925, more than 50,000 members of the Ku Klux Klan paraded through Washington, DC."

He seems perplexed by his own lack of knowledge. Wow, he repeats. As I watch him, I realize I'm seeing what whiteness does to reality or, rather, its memory. The poet Emily Dickinson scribbled on an envelope, "But are not all Facts Dreams as soon as we put them behind us—" No one he encountered—administration, faculty, friends, upperclassmen—thought a cross burning was worth mentioning, important enough to mention, or if it was mentioned, it was not done in such a way as to break open an understanding that would cement it in his memory.

I begin to wonder who among my white college friends knew about the cross burning and still remembers it as part of their college experience and American life. I can count the people I'm still in touch with from college on one hand. I decide to call a close white friend who I think might recollect the moment, but, in all honesty, my expectations are low. This friend remains someone I like to check in with regularly. And, oddly and fortuitously, when I ask her about the cross burning, it turns out she's the one who reported it. She witnessed the act and saw those who carried it out. Perhaps, though I don't remember this, she was the one who told me. Could our closeness in college be attributed in part to an understanding of what remains possible given our history? Even as I held myself at a distance from the event, it remained as part of the landscape in which I passed my college years.

My friend has the pedigree of a WASP. There is natural blond hair, blue eyes, and a family on her father's side that dates back to the time of the *Mayflower*. She knows it, I know it, we all know it the minute we see her. Hers is a world of New England prep schools, our shared formerly gentlemen's college, and Ivy League graduate institutions. We have little in common beyond our schooling,

Text *I wonder if white people don't develop friendships with people of color, especially blacks, because they don't want to be implicated in or confronted by white violence against black people. Imagine going to a black friend's house and sitting down to dinner with a tall glass of lead-tainted water.*

Fact Check Maybe.

Notes and Sources In 2017 a state agency called the Michigan Commission on Civil Rights concluded that systemic racism played a key role in crisis and its subsequent poor management: "The people of Flint have been subjected to unprecedented harm and hardship, much of it caused by structural and systemic discrimination and racism that have corroded your city, your institutions, and your water pipes, for generations."

A recent report in the *Proceedings of the National Academy of Sciences*, "Inequality in Consumption of Goods and Services Adds to Racial-Ethnic Disparities in Air Pollution Exposure," found that black people and nonwhite Hispanics disproportionately breathe air polluted by non-Hispanic white people: "Blacks are more exposed than whites/others to pollution from every emitter group. The same holds for Hispanics, with the exceptions of $PM_{2.5}$ originating from agriculture, from coal electric utilities, and from residential wood combustion, for which they are exposed to 11%, 40%, and 14% less, respectively, than whites/others. Those three types of emissions are concentrated in regions of the United States with relatively low Hispanic populations. Whites/others consume more—and cause more exposure—than blacks and Hispanics across all seven end-use categories" (Christopher W. Tessum et al.).

but still we remain close. She was leaving a Black Student Union party on Homecoming weekend when she encountered the burning cross. That she saw it did not make her conscious of black people since she already had an integrated life, but it no doubt helped to make the conversations between us less work.

I wonder if white people don't develop friendships with people of color, especially blacks, because they don't want to be implicated in or confronted by white violence against black people. Imagine going to a black friend's house and sitting down to dinner with a tall glass of lead-tainted water. I am being fanciful, I know (white people don't need to give black people a thought most of the time), but if I follow this line of logic, I imagine the violence complicates all the misguided aspirations for a postracial anything. Then the white person would have to negotiate actual clear and present danger even as others insist that blacks need to just "rise up." My friend's proximity to predominantly black students at the house party brought her literally face-to-face with white terrorism. I wonder how she processed it all.

What happened? I ask her. What happened, and what were you thinking?

In 1980, when I was a freshman in college, one of my best friends, and the person I roomed with sophomore year, was a black man. We went to a lot of parties together, and one evening we went to a Black Student Union party in one of the dorms on campus. It was open to anyone, so as a white woman, I was welcome. I left the party early, and as I was walking out of the building into the dark of a grassy area next to a stand of trees, I saw two men dressed in white robes running toward the trees. They lit something on fire and a cross that had been put up that evening burst into flames as they

Text *I'm sure it was far more upsetting to the black students.*

Notes and Sources The "Unite the Right" march was organized in response to the growing calls to remove the Confederate statue in the town. That statue was put up in the city of Charlottesville in 1924 (a year before the Klan march in Washington). In February 2016, the city voted to remove it from Lee Park and rename the park. They were sued by organizations called the "Monument Fund" and the "Virginia Division of the Sons of Confederate Veterans," among others. The "Unite the Right" rally was held on August 12, 2017, in response to the statue's planned removal.

ran off. It happened so quickly. I guess I could have chased them, but I ran back inside to where other friends were dancing and started shouting to come look. Everyone rushed to the windows and outside. Someone called security, and I don't actually remember if we waited for security to put out the fire or if someone from the party did. It was such a shock. How could someone who lived in our community be willing to commit an act this offensive and disgusting? How could a group do this together?

As the main witness, I spent time with security describing what I saw. A few days later, I was asked to come to the administration building, where I sat down with some higher-up administrators who showed me a collection of pictures and asked if these were any of the perpetrators. It was dark, it was far away, they had sheets on. There was no way I could identify the men who did this. I was asked to the office a second time to look at another collection of possible perpetrators. Again, I told them I didn't see any faces well enough to identify the people.

I was eighteen. I'm white. But I still understood how offensive and disturbing it was to have people light a cross next to a Black Student Union party. I'm sure it was far more upsetting to the black students. I could move on, but I don't know how other students felt after that. My friend took it in stride. It's just a few stupid guys.

The questions I have asked myself since then:

Instead of running back into the party to point out the cross burning in the yard, should I have run over and tried to put it out, neutering the impact? The burners were trying to offend the BSU partygoers. If no one saw the cross, their planning and efforts would be wasted. But was it important for people to see it? Could I have just told people, and they could have seen the evidence on the lawn—a burnt cross lying on its side? I don't know if that would have been better.

Text *This idea that racism is solely a dynamic of youth and ignorance seems its own form of American optimism.*

Notes and Sources The *GQ* profile by Rachel Kaadzi Ghansah on Dylann Roof describes his online community: "They are young, they are white, and they often brag about their arsenals of guns, because these are the guns that will save them in the coming race war. They are armed to the teeth, and almost always painfully undereducated or somewhat educated but extremely socially awkward. That is, until their eyes are opened to the fact that within the world of white supremacy they can find friends."

Should I have chased the guys to get a better look at who they were? I think I was a little frozen with shock, but maybe I could have gotten a better look at them, identified them, and forced them to leave the community and school.

How did these guys find each other? Did one of them use the N-word at an all-white gathering and watch to see who laughed and who turned away? And then they spent time planning an act whose sole goal was to deeply offend fellow students? And maybe I was sitting in a class with one of these guys the next day. And right now, they are walking around, doing things with their kids, going to work. Do they look back with regret at doing that, now that they are older and wiser, or do they still relish that racist act? Are they cheering on the white nationalist movement?

The next week there was a march on campus to protest the cross burning. I actually think the administration was very disturbed by the crime and handled it well. But it still remained that there were students on campus who spent time and effort planning a cross burning.

As I read my friend's response, I wonder if she really wonders if the perpetrators "look back with regret." This idea that racism is solely a dynamic of youth and ignorance seems its own form of American optimism. She wonders if they are "cheering on the white nationalist movement" rather than if they are white nationalists.

I am surprised at my own melancholic reactions to these final thoughts of hers. This unwillingness to know how deep-seated and deeply felt racism remains is strangely disheartening and distantly alarming. Even here. Even her. I don't want these thoughts to intrude on a friendship I value. Even here. Even her. Then I

National Socialist Movement Rally, Newnan, Georgia, 2018

recall Homi Bhabha from *The Location of Culture*, in conversation with Toni Morrison: "Remembering is never a quiet act of intro-spection or retrospection. It is a painful re-membering, a putting together of the dismembered past to make sense of the trauma of the present." Her unwillingness to entertain the notion that the cross burners are the white nationalists of the present is a way not to see "the trauma of the present" as in a continuum from the past into the future. According to the police reports from the cross burning, former students were persons of interest. What are they doing now? Are they now part of our justice system?

My friend is not alone in her willingness to give the men a pass. The FBI investigation of the college event concluded that the cross burning had probably been a prank, according to a press report at the time. In any case, whoever burned the cross or who-ever was inspired by those that burned the cross continued to harass students connected to the Black Student Union for weeks after the event. According to police records, there were reports of threats generated by someone who was probably inside the col-lege community (given that specific black students were targeted as well as the white president, who was seen as having brought them there). One student received a letter that stated, "You God damned stinkin', Filthy, black skinned Monkies do Not belong among a white human society. You shit colored Animals will even-tually be phased out. In plain English—Eliminated."

The question of what to do with these realities when many black people, graduating from this and other schools with similar oc-currences, go on to achieve successful lives, at times coupled with economic wealth, remains for some an oxymoron. Understanding what is possible on the part of liberal whites means understanding that black personal achievement does not negate the continued

Text *Though all should have been appalled at Clinton's utterance because, intended or not, it seemed "a wing and a prayer," she was not un-American in signaling the possibility. Murdered, assassinated, incarcerated, or abandoned black people are an acceptable loss for many white Americans.*

Notes and Sources Robin DiAngelo, *White Fragility*: "I was raised in a society that taught me that there was no loss in the absence of people of color—that their absence was a good and desirable thing to be sought and maintained—while simultaneously denying the fact. This attitude has shaped every aspect of my self-identity; my interests and investments, what I care about or don't care about, what I see or don't see, what I am drawn to and what I am repelled by, what I can take for granted, where I can go, how others respond to me, and what I can ignore."

James Baldwin, *The Price of the Ticket*: "A mob is not autonomous: it executes the real will of the people who rule the State. . . . The idea of black persons as property, for example, does not come from the mob. It is not a spontaneous idea. It does not come from the people, who knew better . . . this idea comes from the architects of the American State. These architects decided that the concept of Property was more important—more real—than the possibilities of the human being."

assault of white terrorism. When Hillary Clinton refused to pull out of the 2008 Democratic primary despite no apparent way forward, because as she said "we all remember Bobby Kennedy was assassinated in June [1968] in California," she was in fact pointing to the unspoken reality that President Obama's achievements did not safeguard him from white terrorism. Though all should have been appalled at Clinton's utterance because, intended or not, it seemed "a wing and a prayer," she was not un-American in signaling the possibility. Murdered, assassinated, incarcerated, or abandoned black people are an acceptable loss for many white Americans. And though more blacks are killed in neighborhood crimes, those killed or incarcerated by whites often seem targeted simply because of the color of their skin, since the outcome of those interactions often results in anything from oversentencing to death. The indifference is impenetrable and reliable and distributed across centuries, and I am stupidly hurt when my friends can't see that. Perhaps that's my nonwhite fragility.

study on white male privilege

Text *The statistic that leads up to the phrase "white male privilege" being uttered noted the percentage of transgender people likely to be victims of police violence.*

Notes and Sources A 2011 study by the National Center for Transgender Equality and the National Gay and Lesbian Task Force shows: "More than one-fifth (22%) of transgender people who had interacted with police reported police harassment, and 6% of transgender individuals reported that they experienced bias-motivated assault by officers. Black transgender people reported much higher rates of biased harassment and assault (38% and 15%)."

I am attempting to understand why telling a white male that he has benefited from "white male privilege" feels abusive to him. I listen again to the video from a training seminar where police are discussing the treatment of transgender people. The discussion is led by a US Department of Justice representative. The statistic that leads up to the phrase "white male privilege" being uttered ● noted the percentage of transgender people likely to be victims of police violence.

DATA

PLAINFIELD, INDIANA, POLICE CAPTAIN SCOTT ARNDT (responding to statistics of violence against trans people presented by instructor): That's not even accurate, because if you can't have a basis for where the number comes from or what the situation is that puts them in that situation—I mean, are they more likely to be in this situation than somebody who's not transgender?

INSTRUCTOR: Yes.

CAPT. SCOTT ARNDT (interrupting): Which I don't know what that is—I'm just saying my life has never been part of police violence. Most of the people that I know have never been—accused the police of violence. So I guess I don't get where that statistic comes from.

PLAINFIELD POLICE CAPTAIN CARRI WEBER (from audience, off camera): 'Cause of your white male privilege, so you wouldn't know.

Plainfield, Indiana, Police Department

CAPT. SCOTT ARNDT: I'm sorry?

CAPT. WEBER: Your white male privilege.

INSTRUCTOR: Let's bring it down a notch.

FACILITATOR: Let's keep it safe and professional. That's my [he is interrupted here and then continues] role and I don't want to focus on the statistics, because quite frankly—

CAPT. SCOTT ARNDT (interrupting): Chief, you gonna let [unintelligible] get away with that? Seriously? I'm asking a legitimate question here, and I'm getting [unintelligible] white privilege? Are you serious? [yelling] I find that extremely offensive.

[There is an additional back-and-forth between these two comments.]

FACILITATOR: We're not talking about white privilege here. We're trying to focus on a different demographic. I'm gonna keep this professional, and I apologize if anyone is offended.

END OF DATA

RESULTS

In the Scott Arndt video of the actual incident, Arndt states that he heard the phrase "white male privilege" as "extremely offensive." In the complaint he filed, he states that he was "racially and

sexistly slurred." The white female police captain Weber, who used the phrase, was put on paid administrative leave. A closed executive session ultimately issued her a letter of reprimand and reinstated her.

When the white male officer hears the phrase "white male privilege" used to describe him, he demonstrates white male rage. He was punished with a two-day suspension without pay. Though the rage is questioned, no one explicitly associates it with white male privilege; hence the letter of reprimand in Weber's file. Surely, Arndt must understand himself as white and male, so perhaps it's the noun "privilege" that enrages him? But a "racial slur" means you refer to his whiteness in an offensive way. The association of whiteness with privilege therefore must offend.

Does he know that privilege, a word first used in the twelfth century, referred to a "bill of law in favor of or against an individual"? That the laws favor him as a white male must remain a known unknown. He cannot bear to know it and know that he accommodates and makes visible all that has been redirected toward him. He cannot bear the burden of what was taken to be given to him. He cannot know himself as the embodied space of privilege even as he becomes its evidence. He will not know himself as the favored even as he destroys others in order not to know. Even as person after person lives dependent on him, waiting for him, looking to him to know what he cannot—or is it will not?—know.

tall

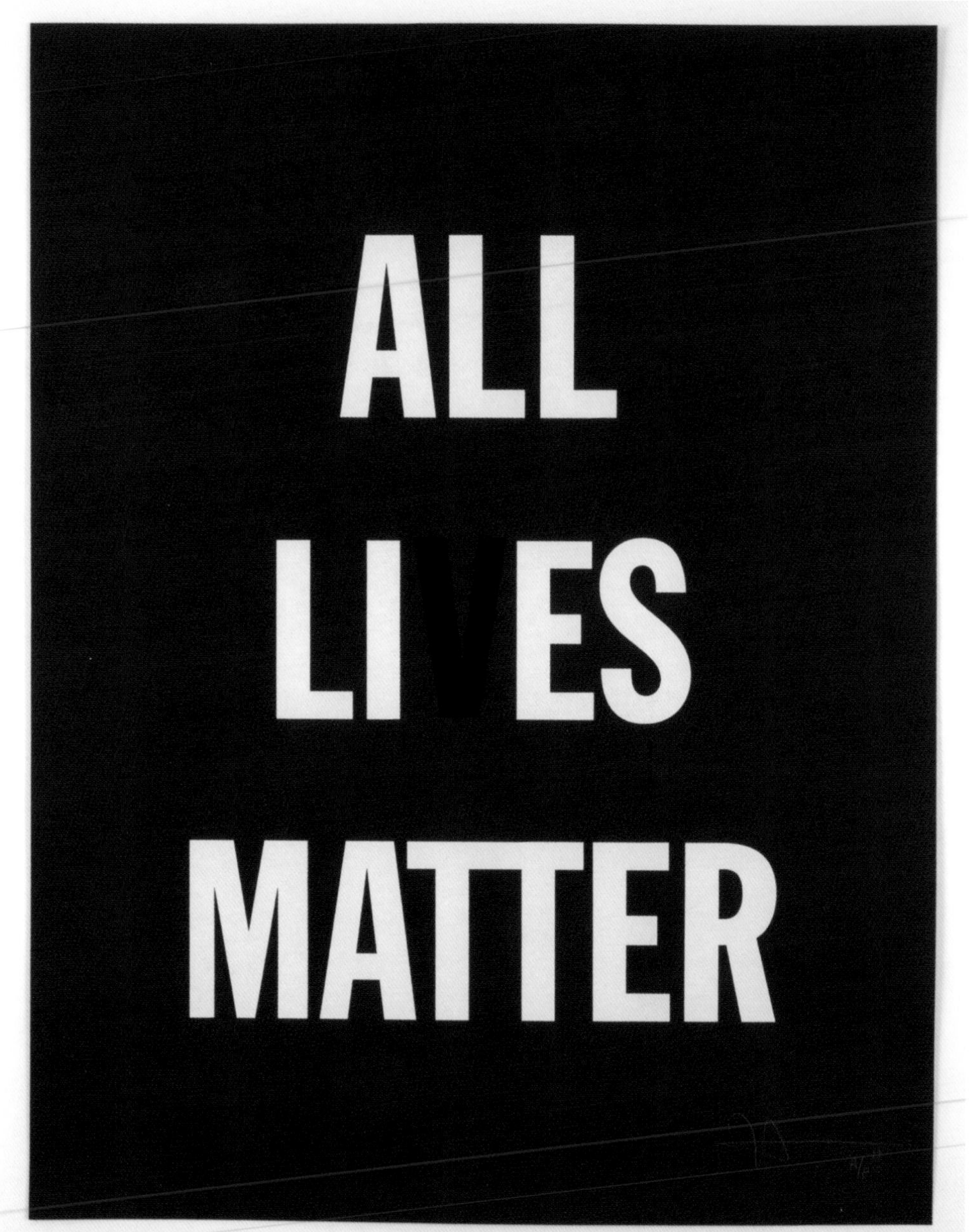
ALL
LIVES
MATTER

On my way to retrieve my coat I'm paused in the hallway in someone else's home when a man approaches to tell me he thinks his greatest privilege is his height. There's a politics around who is tallest, and right now he's passively blocking passage, so yes. But greatest, no. Predictably, I say, I think your whiteness is your greatest privilege. To this, he pivots and reports that, unlike other whites who have confessed to him they are scared of blacks, he is comfortable around black people because he played basketball. He doesn't say with black men because that's implied. For no good reason, except perhaps inside the inane logic of if you like something so much, you might as well marry it, I ask him, are you married to a black woman? What? He says, no, she's Jewish. After a pause, he adds, she's white. I don't ask him about his closest friends, his colleagues, his neighbors, his wife's friends, his institutions, our institutions, structural racism, weaponized racism, ignorant racism, internalized racism, unconscious bias—I just decide, since nothing keeps happening, no new social inter- action, no new utterances from me or him, both of us in default fantasies, I just decide to stop tilting my head to look up. I have again reached the end of waiting. What is it the theorist Saidiya Hartman said? "Educating white people about racism has failed." Or, was it that "hallways are liminal zones where we shouldn't fail to see what's possible." Either way, and still, all the way home, the tall man's image stands before me, ineluctable. And then the Hartman quote I am searching for arrives: "One of the things I think is true, which is a way of thinking about the afterlife of slavery in regard to how we inhabit historical time, is the sense of temporal entanglement, where the past, the present and the future, are not discrete and cut off from one another, but rather that we live the simultaneity of that entanglement. This is almost common sense for black folk. How does one narrate that?" Her question is the hoop that encircles.

social contract

Text *It's my belief antiblack and anti-Latinx racism couched in the terms "Obamacare" and "immigration" and "the wall" was the mighty engine . . .*

Notes and Sources One major study that supports the argument that race was a determining factor in the election is John Sides, Michael Tesler, and Lynn Vavreck's *Identity Crisis: The 2016 Presidential Campaign and the Battle for the Meaning of America*: "Another and arguably even more important element of the context is political actors. They help articulate the content of a group identity, or what it means to be part of a group. Political actors also identify, and sometimes exaggerate or even invent, threats to a group. Political actors can then make group identities and attitudes more salient and elevate them as criteria for decision-making."

Text *. . . the very president who refers to himself as a nationalist.*

Notes and Sources "Trump Says He's a 'Nationalist,'" by Neeti Upadhye: https://www.nytimes.com/video/us/politics/100000006175744/trump-nationalist.html

USA Today, "'I'm a Nationalist': Trump's Embrace of Controversial Label Sparks Uproar": "You know, they have a word—it's sort of become old-fashioned—it's called a nationalist. And I say, really, we're not supposed to use that word. You know what I am? I'm a nationalist, okay? I'm a nationalist. Nationalist. Nothing wrong. Use that word. Use that word."

Text *. . . "many factors" are the rhetorical tide I swim upstream against, as if George Wallace hadn't attributed his political success to the articulation of racist rhetoric.*

Fact Check Yes. Wallace attributed his political rise to racist rhetoric and policy but not specifically his four terms as governor. See below.

Notes and Sources See Dan T. Carter's biography of George Wallace, *The Politics of Rage*: "Wallace shrugged. 'I started off talking about schools and highways and prisons and taxes—and I couldn't make them listen,' he told Louis Eckl, editor of the *Florence Times*. 'Then I began talking about niggers—and they stomped the floor.'"

I'm at a dinner where the "whys and wherefores" of the 2016 presidential election come up, because they do, and one guest, it turns out, is writing a book. In the description of the book the role of racism is barely mentioned. Hold up. It's my belief anti-black and anti-Latinx racism couched in the terms "Obamacare" and "immigration" and "the wall" was the mighty engine that brought our current president to power, the very president who refers to himself as a nationalist. The generic and deracialized "many factors" are the rhetorical tide I swim upstream against, as if George Wallace hadn't attributed his political success to the articulation of racist rhetoric. Despite his declared neutral feelings about black people, Wallace ran on "segregation now, segregation tomorrow, segregation forever" and promised to protect the Anglo-Saxon Southland. What exactly has changed?

There was no way to predict that white Democrats who had voted for President Obama would vote in key states for a fascist regime, is the persistent retort. Our resident expert added that he didn't have a crystal ball, as if unarmed dead black people weren't lying in our American streets or white people weren't calling the police on black people without cause, with full knowledge of all the ways that could go wrong and end in the loss of a life. And as if our forty-fifth president before his official run hadn't been vocal about the lie that voters had been duped by a president who wasn't born in America.

My dogged insistence meant I was sailing closer and closer to the trope of the angry black woman. I wasn't completely right—there were the Russians, the Electoral College, and misogyny—but I needed these people to understand I would rather be wrong, would gladly join them in the perception of an unpredictable world if I could. Perhaps.

Text *It's harder than you would think because white people don't really want change if it means they need to think differently than they do about who they are.*

Fact Check Yes, but just to note—there may be counterexamples.

Notes and Sources Ashley Jardina's work may be of interest: "When the dominant status of whites relative to racial and ethnic minorities is secure and unchallenged, white identity likely remains dormant. When whites perceive their group's dominant status is threatened or their group is unfairly disadvantaged, however, their racial identity may become salient and politically relevant."

Self-Presentation in Interracial Settings: *The Competence Downshift by White Liberals*, by Cydney Dupree and Susan T. Fiske: "White liberals self-present less competence to minorities than to other Whites—that is, they patronize minorities stereotyped as lower status and less competent. . . . This possibly unintentional but ultimately patronizing competence-downshift suggests that well-intentioned liberal Whites may draw on low-status/competence stereotypes to affiliate with minorities."

I learned early that being right pales next to staying in the room. All kinds of things happen as the night unfolds. But sometimes I become caught by the idea that repetition occurs if the wheels keep spinning. Repetition is insistence and one can collude only so much. Sometimes I just want to throw myself inside the gears. Sometimes, as James Baldwin said, I want to change one word or a single sentence. It's harder than you would think because white people don't really want change if it means they need to think differently than they do about who they are. We have a precedent in Eartha Kitt, who after confronting Lady Bird and Lyndon Johnson about Vietnam at a luncheon at the White House was blacklisted. Democrats all. Whiteness wants the kind of progress that reflects what it values, a reflection of itself. Voter suppression is about racism; immigration issues and DACA are informed by racism. I am saying this and I am saying that, and, as if I have suddenly become too much, a metaphorical white hand reaches out to pull me back into the fold from the perilous edge of angry black womanhood.

A white woman effectively ends the conversation on 45's campaign tactics by turning our gaze toward the dessert tray. How beautiful, she says. Homemade brownies on a silver tray? Hers is the fey gesture I have seen exhibited so often by white women in old movies—women who are overcome by shiny objects. It's so blatant a redirect I can't help but ask aloud the most obvious question: Am I being silenced?

I'm aware my question breaks the rules of social engagement. I'm aware I will never be invited back to this house, back into the circle of these white people. I understand inadvertently causing someone to feel shame isn't cool. But: Am I being silenced?

Text *As I sit there listening to these polite white people discuss this, I realize the history of experimenting on black people does not hold a place in their referential memory.*

Notes and Sources Harriet A. Washington, *Medical Apartheid: The Dark History of Medical Experimentation on Black Americans from Colonial Times to the Present*: "The Office for Protection from Research Risks (OPRR) has been busily investigating abuses at more than sixty research centers, including experimentation-related deaths at premier universities, from Columbia to California. Another important subset of human subject abuse has been scientific fraud, wherein scientists from the University of South Carolina to MIT have also been found to have lied through falsified data or fictitious research agendas, often in the service of research that abused black Americans. Within recent years, the OPRR has also suspended research at such revered universities as Alabama, Pennsylvania, Duke, Yale, and even Johns Hopkins."

Linda Villarosa, "Myths about Physical Racial Differences Were Used to Justify Slavery—and Are Still Believed by Doctors Today," the 1619 Project, the *New York Times Magazine*: "Over the centuries, the two most persistent physiological myths—that black people were impervious to pain and had weak lungs that could be strengthened through hard work—wormed their way into scientific consensus, and they remain rooted in modern-day medical education and practice. In the 1787 manual *A Treatise on Tropical Diseases; and on the Climate of the West-Indies*, a British doctor, Benjamin Moseley, claimed that black people could bear surgical operations much more than white people, noting that 'what would be the cause of insupportable pain to a white man, a Negro would almost disregard.' To drive home his point, he added, 'I have amputated the legs of many Negroes who have held the upper part of the limb themselves.'"

I wanted this white woman to look me in the eye and say, Yes. Yes, you are. I wanted her to own her action and not cower. I would have liked her then. Instead, all of us around the table have to watch her sink into her seat as she looks down at her hands as if I've refused to shake them. Now the others have to take sides. White solidarity needs to be reestablished. It's then I understand I forfeited the game the minute I stepped into a house where I am the only black person.

The woman and I could have started conversing, instead of one of us using language to erase the next moment. Doesn't she see that, even as a white woman, she remains subject to the arbitrary power of our executive branch? Shouldn't we get clear on how we got here? Or are alliances set? Does she see my insistence as its own form of erasure, or is white civility simply being put to work to maintain the fiction of white benevolence and the uncouthness of blackness?

As I wonder if it's time to leave, in order to restore my own and the dinner's equilibrium, someone else steers the conversation, consciously or unconsciously, away from the brownies to a gentler way of speaking about race. Race and children. The question at hand is whether a child study center should delete the word "study" from its title. The center is located in a city with a sizable black population. The dominant feeling around the table seems to be that the concern over the name is frivolous—the center is attached to an academic institution after all, where all is done in the name of study and research.

As I sit there listening to these polite white people discuss this, I realize the history of experimenting on black people does not hold a place in their referential memory. No one makes mention

Text *... experiments of mustard gas on black soldiers, among other nonwhites ...*

Fact Check Yes. The military did conduct mustard gas experiments on black, white, and other nonwhite soldiers. See below.

Notes and Sources "Secret World War II Chemical Experiments Tested Troops by Race," by Caitlin Dickerson on NPR's *Morning Edition*: "White enlisted men were used as scientific control groups. Their reactions were used to establish what was 'normal,' and then compared to the minority troops."

Text *In "Sexism—a Problem with a Name," Sara Ahmed writes ...*

Notes and Sources Sara Ahmed also addresses impressions in the introduction to *The Cultural Politics of Emotion*: "To form an impression might involve acts of perception and cognition as well as an emotion. But forming an impression also depends on how objects impress upon us. An impression can be an effect on the subject's feelings ('she made an impression'). It can be a belief ('to be under an impression'). It can be an imitation or an image ('to create an impression'). Or it can be a mark on the surface ('to leave an impression'). We need to remember the 'press' in impression. It allows us to associate the experience of having an emotion with the very affect of one surface upon another, an affect that leaves its mark or trace. So not only do I have an impression of others, but they also leave me with an impression; they impress me, and impress upon me."

of Tuskegee's syphilis experiments on black men, or the military experiments of mustard gas on black soldiers, among other non-whites, or J. Marion Sims's experimentation on black women. No mention of Henrietta Lacks. My historical memory starts tossing examples at me as if it's having its own dinner party. In the real one, no one wonders what the parents of the black children think when they see the word "study" associated with the center.

Knowing that my silence is active in the room, I stay silent because I want to make a point of that silence. Among white people, black people are allowed to talk about their precarious lives, but they are not allowed to implicate the present company in that precariousness. They are not allowed to point out its causes. In "Sexism—a Problem with a Name," Sara Ahmed writes that "if you name the problem you become the problem." To create discomfort by pointing out facts is seen as socially unacceptable. Let's get over ourselves, it's structural not personal, I want to shout at everyone, including myself.

But all the structures and all the diversity planning put in place to alter those structures, and all the desires of whites to assimilate blacks in their day-to-day lives, come with the continued outrage at rage. All the perceived outrage at me, the guest who brings all of herself to dinner, all of it—her body, her history, her fears, her furious fears, her expectations—is, in the end, so personal. The mutual anxieties and angers blow invisible in the room. A wind. Blustery, turbulent, squally, overcast: find a discomfort level. I push my brownie around my plate. I am middle-aged and overweight. I shouldn't eat this. I shouldn't eat anything. Nothing.

Moments like these make me understand that the noncomprehension of what is known on the part of whiteness is an active

investment in not wanting to know if that involves taking into account the lives of people of color. And the perceived tiresome insistence on presenting one's knowledge on the part of blackness might be a fruitless and childish exercise. Do I believe either of these positions enough to change my ways? Might as well stop weather from coming.

Had the woman who admired the dessert tray, in an attempt to redirect the conversation, said to me, Here's your coat. What's your hurry? Now, that would have made me smile—the corners of my mouth would have lifted and raised my cheeks to form crow's feet around my eyes. I would have smiled with my eyes in admiration of her directness—get out—rather than serving up redirection and false civility.

violent

Text *Wondering what goes on in the imagination of the Asian boy who also attends this diverse preschool, I decide one possibility could be that he has been read "Goldilocks and the Three Bears" so many times his visual memory was assaulted.*

Notes and Sources Response to a request for permission to use an illustration of a traditional image of "Goldilocks and the Three Bears":

Hi xxxx,
Thanks for sending on the text that you wanted xxxxx's illustration of "Goldilocks and the Three Bears" to accompany. We appreciate being able to read the article and found it very interesting. We have decided, however, that we would prefer not to have this illustration accompany that article.

We wish you the best of luck in finding an illustrator who will want their image used in this way—perhaps it will be easier to find an image available in the public domain.

Best wishes,
xxxx and xxxxxxx

A white friend, who's aware I'm writing on perceptions of whiteness, phones to recount an interaction she just had with her child. I have questioned her on previous occasions regarding how whiteness is talked about in her family, in her home, in her world. She is white, her husband is white, and their child is white. This day her young son returned home from school upset. An Asian boy told him he "ruined" his drawing of "Goldilocks and the Three Bears" by coloring Goldilocks's skin brown. Her son knows there are also people in his world with brown skin. My friend assures her son that he has nothing to worry about.

One thing I thought about since we talked is his preschool. We'd moved here when he was three and we wanted him to have a diverse classroom. So his teacher who he had for nearly two years was East Indian and the class was diverse. Also, the director of the preschool was black. I don't know if this had any impact on why he colored Goldilocks brown, but I do think it impacted his reaction to his classmate's comment that he'd ruined her. My son felt hurt and confused. I think he colored Goldilocks brown because he sees it as an artistic option, a way to represent the world. This year for Christmas when given the choice to paint his ceramic Santa, he opted to paint him black. I didn't ask him why.

Wondering what goes on in the imagination of the Asian boy who also attends this diverse preschool, I decide one possibility could be that he has been read "Goldilocks and the Three Bears" so many times his visual memory was assaulted. The brown crayon represented Goldilocks differently from her normal portrayal, despite my friend's son's attention to her blond hair. But can we say she is ruined? My friend's curiosity is no doubt piqued by whether or not the Asian boy objected based on what he knows about the text or what he knows about the world we share. Ruined? Has anyone explained color-blind casting to him? I jokingly ask my

Text *I am suddenly flooded by a memory of all the doll tests done over the years based on psychologists Dr. Kenneth and Mamie Clark's doll tests, the results of which were used in* Brown v. Board of Education of Topeka *to show the adverse effect of racism on black children, but what about the adverse effects on white children?*

Fact Check Yes.

Notes and Sources K. B. Clark, "Effect of Prejudice and Discrimination on Personality Development" (paper presented at the Midcentury White House Conference on Children and Youth, 1950), as cited in the *Brown v. Board of Education* decision, footnote 11. Clark discusses the specific document cited in that footnote in his book *Prejudice and the Child.* That entire introductory chapter gives an excellent fine-grained overview of the exact submissions attorneys for the plaintiff made to the court. The historian of science John P. Jackson conducts a thorough review of the Clarks' research and Kenneth's testimony in the cases leading up to *Brown* in his book *Social Scientists for Social Justice: Making the Case against Segregation*. See Harvard law professor Lani Guinier's article "From Racial Liberalism to Racial Literacy: *Brown v. Board of Education* and the Interest-Divergence Dilemma" for an examination of the "discontinuity between *Brown*'s early promise and its present reality"; Guinier includes a review of the role the Clarks' research played in the case: "It is an open question whether any legal analysis, even one grounded in more rigorous social science research or employing a more balanced assessment of segregation's causes and effects, could have accomplished the goals of the *Brown* attorneys or could now accomplish the massive tasks that still await us: to extirpate a complex system of relationships that have tortured this country from its earliest beginnings and then to refashion a new social and economic order in its place."

Jane Elliott, "Blue Eyes, Brown Eyes": "What we call education is really indoctrination into white supremacy. I want every white person who could be happy to receive the same treatment as black people to stand. . . . Nobody standing? This means you know what is happening."

friend. But since wondering, as Emily Dickinson would tell us, "is not precisely Knowing and not precisely Knowing not," we don't jump to any conclusions about the boy because context is everything.

I mention to my friend that children's ideas about race are formed by the time they arrive in kindergarten and their racial bias is not random. Social psychologist Kristina Olson makes the claim that "by 3 or 4 years of age, White children in the U.S., Canada, Australia, and Europe show preferences for other White children." This, she says, happens because no matter what we tell children, they model their behavior after their surroundings. Erin Winkler agrees: "As children become more aware of societal norms that favor certain groups over others, they will often show a bias toward the socially privileged group." I am suddenly flooded by a memory of all the doll tests done over the years based on psychologists Dr. Kenneth and Mamie Clark's doll tests, the results of which were used in *Brown v. Board of Education of Topeka* to show the adverse effect of racism on black children, but what about the adverse effects on white children? Or Asian children? Should we care about that?

Text *Winkler's argument is also supported by the work of psychologists Phyllis Katz and Jennifer Kofkin in their 1997 article "Race, Gender, and Young Children." They followed black and white children . . .*

Notes and Sources P. A. Katz and J. A. Kofkin, "Race, Gender, and Young Children": "Some researchers have found that young children prefer same-race peers (Finkelstein & Haskins, 1983; Newman, Liss, & Sherman,1983), although most report a preference for ethnic majority group members and a bias against dark skin colors (e.g., Jaffe, 1988; Porter, 1991; Spencer & Markstrom-Adams, 1990)." In S. S. Luthar et al., *Developmental Psychopathology: Perspectives on Adjustment, Risk, and Disorder.*

Text *It's difficult to be hopeful when even the "eye gaze patterns" of teachers in preschool tend to target black children, especially boys, at the sign of any disturbance in the classroom.*

Notes and Sources A 2016 study by the Yale Child Center, "Do Early Educators' Implicit Biases Regarding Sex and Race Relate to Behavior Expectations and Recommendations of Preschool Expulsions and Suspensions?": "Our findings demonstrate that early education staff tend to observe more closely Blacks, and especially Black boys when challenging behaviors are expected. These findings are important to consider given that no behavioral challenges were present in the videos, suggesting, in part, that preschool teachers may hold differential expectations of challenging behaviors based on the race of the child. . . . Of note, these eye-tracking results closely corresponded with participants' conscious appraisal of which child they felt required the most of their attention, with Black boys being endorsed as requiring the most attention by 42% of early education staff (68% more than expected by chance alone). Additionally, boys in general, were endorsed as requiring the most attention by 76% of early education staff (52% more than expected by chance alone), consistent with research showing that boys (regardless of race) are at greater risk for classroom removal."

Winkler's argument is also supported by the work of psychologists Phyllis Katz and Jennifer Kofkin in their 1997 article "Race, Gender, and Young Children." They followed black and white children and, according to Winkler, "found that all of the children expressed an in-group bias at the age of 30 months. When asked to choose a potential playmate from among photos of unfamiliar white and black boys and girls, all of the children chose a samerace playmate. However, by 36 months, the majority of both black and white children chose white playmates . . . and this pattern held at the 60-month mark, although it decreased slightly at that point." I wonder if parents who agreed to their children's involvement in the study were surprised by the results. Social bias, according to psychologists Danielle Perszyk, Ryan F. Lei, Galen V. Bodenhausen, Jennifer A. Richeson, and Sandra R. Waxman, becomes more difficult to change once the children get older.

How does one combat the racism of a culture? It's difficult to be hopeful when even the "eye gaze patterns" of teachers in preschool tend to target black children, especially boys, at the sign of any disturbance in the classroom. One wonders how this could not become a social cue for all the children.

Another friend who is black tells me the director of her son's private school called to tell her her son was put out of the class for his behaviors. In the ensuing exchange the school director describes the four-year-old as violent. Violent? He threw a puzzle piece and he pulled the teacher's hair when she removed him from the room. He had a meltdown. Violent, my friend keeps repeating. He is four years old. Did you tell his teachers there are words besides incompetent that can frame their use of the word "violent"? I ask.

Text *When she removed her son from the school, his white teacher cried because there should be no consequences to the school staff's reading of black boyhood as violent.*

Notes and Sources Phillip Atiba Goff, Matthew Christian Jackson, Brooke Allison Lewis Di Leone, Carmen Marie Culotta, and Natalie Ann DiTomasso, "The Essence of Innocence: Consequences of Dehumanizing Black Children," *Journal of Personality and Social Psychology*: "Because dehumanization involves the denial of full humanness to others (Haslam, 2006), one would expect a reduction of social considerations offered to humans for those who are dehumanized. This reduction violates one defining character-istic of children—being innocent and thus needing protection—rendering the category 'children' less essential and distinct from adults."

Text *Was I being ungenerous in my dismissal of the teacher's feelings? She cried because emotionally she was sad about what was happening.*

Notes and Sources Robin DiAngelo, *White Fragility*: "Consequently, if we whites want to interrupt this system, we have to get racially *uncomfortable* and to be willing to examine the effects of our racial engagement. This includes not indulging in whatever reactions we have—anger, defensiveness, self-pity, and so forth—in a given cross-racial encounter without first reflecting on what is driving our reactions and how they will affect other people. Tears that are driven by white guilt are self-indulgent. When we are mired in guilt, we are narcissistic and ineffective; guilt functions as an excuse for inaction. Further, because we so seldom have authentic and sustained cross-racial relationships, our tears do not feel like solidarity to people of color we have not previously supported. Instead, our tears function as impotent reflexes that don't lead to constructive action. We need to reflect on when we cry and when we don't, and why."

The feminist, queer, and postcolonial theorist Sara Ahmed writes in "The Phenomenology of Whiteness," "To give a problem a name can change not only *how* we register an event but *whether* we register an event. To give the problem a name can be experienced as *magnifying the problem*; allowing something to acquire a social and physical density by gathering up what otherwise remain scattered experiences into a *tangible thing*." My friend laughs, but says she just wants her child to be in a safe space where he is allowed to have developmentally appropriate toddler tantrums and yet be helped to deal with his emotions in a compassionate way. If you don't name what's happening, everyone can pretend it's not happening, I say, somewhat annoyed. I know, she says, but those white women are not my concern. When she removed her son from the school, his white teacher cried because there should be no consequences to the school staff's reading of black boyhood as violent. Violent. Help. Help.

After I hang up with this friend, I wonder at my own irritation. It is not simply about the white director's use of the word violent. It is also about what I perceive to be my friend's passivity. Maybe she didn't push the moment to its crisis because she saw the white woman's tears as a concession of some sort. Was I being ungenerous in my dismissal of the teacher's feelings? She cried because she was sad about what was happening. Even if the tears are motivated by a sense of persecution rather than guilt, they are still tears, my therapist points out. Is there no room for her to be more than one thing? I am taken aback by this question. But why do I need to perform something she couldn't perform for a four-year-old? Am I supposed to give the benefit of the doubt to an adult who can't give it to a child? Nothing is suspended for her, even given my inability to take her tears into account, and still I must take her tears into account. The tears signify a failure

2010 video stills from CNN

perhaps, a sense of failure perhaps, or is it a sense of victimhood or a sense of guilt, maybe; but I can't be sure the teacher knows she's the one who failed my friend's child (rather than my friend failing her) unless we name the failure. I can't be sure, but how I read the tears is less important than acknowledging that they communicate some kind of emotional understanding or lack of understanding, my therapist tells me. I ask my friend what she was thinking faced with the tears of the white teacher.

White female fragility and victimhood are the first two things that came to mind. But I didn't have the time or energy to focus on that. In that moment, I was fighting for control of my son's educational well-being and the narrative that was being spun already at four. I knew that from a research and intellectual perspective this stuff happened, but when you're actually experiencing it, you are in survival mode. I knew that I needed to find teachers who understood young children's social and emotional development and who also had a deeper awareness of how white supremacy reigns and manifests in preschool, where the rates of suspension and expulsion are greater than they are for youth in K–12.

Fortunately, I found a new preschool and teachers who got it. They comprehend the inherent danger in labeling young Black boys, and they also understand that didn't have to adultify my four-year-old . . . that he is a young child, an evolving and not fully socialized human being just like his white peers in the new classroom. It's not that he doesn't still have tantrums and doesn't need guidance. "They all have something to work on!" the new teachers exclaimed when I shared my now heightened concerns about the tantrums (based on the prior experiences in the old school).

As they spoke to me openly and explicitly about racial bias in schools, especially against Black boys, and talked from their personal experiences,

2010 video stills from CNN

I knew that I had potentially found some dream keepers—teachers with a deep awareness of how our racist, classist, sexist society works and whose express desire is to keep the hopes and dreams alive for all children through effective teaching, sharing, caring, and loving.

So no, I don't think about that white teacher with the tears, or the school director whose anger I fueled because I pointed out the inherent violence in her description of my four-year-old as violent. I couldn't give a damn. What this experience has taught me is that I will have to be vigilant for the rest of his school years, and I lament the fact that parents with less means don't have the privilege of making choices that I do.

Shiiiiiiiiiiiiiiiiit, you can't win for losing. I am suddenly Bunk Moreland from David Simon's *The Wire* as I recount my friend's story about her son to a woman who jolts me out of Bunk's saying. Or is she locking me into it when she reminds me of the twelve-year-old black girls who were allegedly "evaluated" by their school nurse in a manner described to be like those who are strip-searched. The girls were said to be "hyper and giddy" when they exhibited too much laughter, too much joy, too much levity in their Binghamton, New York, middle school, so were then asked to strip down because joy is too much and the tantrums are violent and the skin is too dark and the blackness is unbearable.

Or, as Fred Moten has written in his description of blackness for Erica R. Edwards, Roderick A. Ferguson, and Jeffery O. G. Ogbar's *Keywords for African American Studies*, "The analysis of our murderer, and of our murder, is so we can see we are not murdered. We survive. And then, as we catch a sudden glimpse of ourselves, we shudder. For we are shattered. Nothing survives. The nothingness we share is all that's real. That's what we come

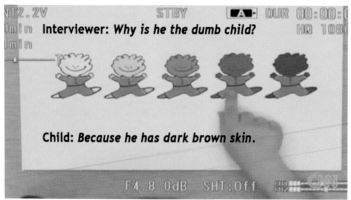

2010 video stills from CNN

out to show. That showing is, or ought to be, our constant study." Study, yes, but the life of it also remains a constant negotiation. Is the harassment of black children by grown people an inability to contain their irritation at our survival? What did Adrian Piper say? "Everything will be taken away." And still we remain demanding a little R&R: Reparations and Reconstruction.

sound and fury

Text *White portraits on white walls signal ownership of all, even as white walls white in.*

Notes and Sources Abigail Cain, "How the White Cube Came to Dominate the Art World": "But it wasn't until the Third Reich took hold of the country during the 1930s that white became *the* standardized color for German gallery walls. 'In England and France white only becomes a dominant wall colour in museums after the Second World War, so one is almost tempted to speak of the white cube as a Nazi invention,' [Charlotte] Klonk said. 'At the same time, the Nazis also mobilized the traditional connotation of white as a colour of purity, but this played no role when the flexible white exhibition container became the default mode for displaying art in the museum.'"

Elena Filipovic, "The Global White Cube": "Particular to the white cube is that it operates under the pretense that its seeming invisibility allows the artwork best to speak; it seems blank, innocent, unspecific, insignificant. Ultimately, what makes a white cube a white cube is that, in our experience of it, ideology and form meet, and all without our noticing it. Years after Barr invoked the white cube as the hallmark of the MoMA's exhibition spaces, Hitler approved of its use for the interior of the Haus der Kunst in Munich in 1937, the Nazis' first architectural project after coming to power. That monumental new building with its interior of vast well-lit gallery spaces, all white and windowless, opened with the exhibition *Grosse deutsche Kunstausstellung* (Great German Art Exhibition). The white container and sober display served to make the painted idyllic landscapes and bronze Aryan bodies on view seem natural and innocuous, despite the belligerent motives that underlay their selection and presentation. Driving home the point, the demonstration was doubly staged; *Grosse deutsche Kunstausstellung* was the 'acceptable,' positive pendant to the somber, densely cluttered, and apparently disorganized show *Entartete Kunst* (Degenerate Art) that opened in a nearby archeological institute the following day. Thanks to such a contrast, the artworks in the former seemed all the more righteous and those in the latter all the more abhorrent. There is no denying the coincidence: When the aestheticization of politics reached terrifying proportions, the white cube was called in. New York and Munich, 1929 and 1937."

The gloom is

the off-white of white. Because white can't know

what white knows. Where's the life in that?
Where's the right in that? Where's the white in that?

At the bone of bone white breathes the fear of being,
the frustration of seeming unequal to white.

White portraits on white walls signal ownership of all,
even as white walls white in.

And this is understandable, yes,

understandable because the culture claims white

is owed everything—a wealth of inheritance
a system insures. In each generation

the equation holds—and better than
before and indifferent to now and enough

and always and inevitably white.

This is what it means to wear a color and believe

its touch an embrace. Even without luck

or chance of birth the scaffolding has rungs
and legacy and the myth of meritocracy fixed in white.

Text *Who implies white could disown its own even as white won't strike its own structure.*

Notes and Sources Caroline Randall Williams, "You Want a Confederate Monument? My Body Is a Confederate Monument": "If there are those who want to remember the legacy of the Confederacy, if they want monuments, well, then, my body is a monument. My skin is a monument."

That's how white holds itself together

as the days hold so many white would not—

White is living within brick-and-mortar, walling off
all others' loss, exhaustion, aggrieved
exposure, dispossessed despair—

in daylight white hardens its features.

Eyes, which hold all light, harden.
Jaws, closing down on justice,
harden into a fury that will not call

white to account even as for some
its pledge is cut out from under.

If people could just come clean about their lives,
even as poverty exists inside white walls,
and just being white is what's working.

Who implies white could disown its own
even as white won't strike its own structure.

Even as white won't oust its own system.

All redress fuels nothing the second another
can be thrown out.

In daylight white's right to righteous rage
doubles down on the supremacy
of white in our way.

big little lies

Text *This claim hasn't completely left my lips before I'm stalled by the thought that I have no inherited wealth . . .*

Notes and Sources Darrick Hamilton and William A. Darity Jr.'s 2017 article "The Political Economy of Education, Financial Literacy, and the Racial Wealth Gap" argues that "inheritance, bequest, and in vivo transfer account for more of the racial wealth gap than any other behavioral, demographic, or socioeconomic indicator. . . . The intergenerational racial wealth gap was structurally created and has virtually nothing to do with individual or racialized *choices*. The source of inequality is structural, not behavioral—intrafamily transfers provide some young adults with the capital to purchase a wealth-generating asset such as a home, a new business, or a debt-free college education that will appreciate over a lifetime. Access to this non-merit-based seed money is not based on some action or inaction on the part of the individual, but rather the familial position into which they are born."

Text *. . . but typically, even if we arrived in the same dorm room, we don't actually wind up in the same place economically, since whites have ten times the net worth of blacks.*

Fact Check Yes. According to Pew and Brandeis University's Institute on Assets and Social Policy, in 2016 the median wealth of white households was ten times the median wealth of black households.

Notes and Sources Pew: "In 2019, the median wealth of white households was $171,000. That's 10 times the wealth of black households ($17,150)." Tom Shapiro, director of the Institute on Assets and Social Policy, confirmed these figures via email.

I'm speaking to a white friend about the class breakdown in the television series *Big Little Lies*. Economic stability or instability gets communicated by the size and location of the different characters' homes. My friend and I live in similar houses, with comparable layouts and approximately the same square footage. This is, perhaps, why I make the careless mistake of putting us in the same class category as Reese Witherspoon's character in the show. I say we are represented by the couple whose nice house doesn't overlook anything—water, cliff, or any other natural wonder.

This claim hasn't completely left my lips before I'm stalled by the thought that I have no inherited wealth; I didn't have a choice ● about whether to work outside the home while raising my child as my friend did, and, and . . .

I recant as quickly as I'd claimed the twinning based on the similarity of our homes' layouts. It's an odd error to have made, but my friend and I do have lives that look similar: both of us are writers with equivalent educational backgrounds, life traumas, and aspirations for ourselves and our families. We have known each other much of our adult lives, and perhaps affection and familiarity made me momentarily oblivious to our differences.

Our economic histories point in part to our racial histories—not that there aren't individual blacks wealthier than my friend, but typically, even if we arrived in the same dorm room, we don't ac- ● tually wind up in the same place economically, since whites have a median net worth that is ten times that of blacks. Our different races have positioned us in the world in radically different ways—her wealth goes back to the *Mayflower*, and her white Anglo-Saxon positioning is how she explains many things about her life. My own immigration from a previously colonized country, naturalized American citizenship, and status as a first-generation

Text *Any attempt to erase these differences ultimately destabilizes us, because, despite our many connections, despite sitting across from each other, we have been pushed out of a structure from opposing ends, through the doorway of our shared culture, to sit across from each other.*

Notes and Sources

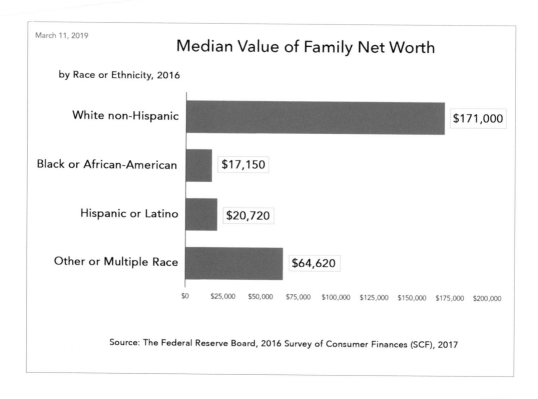

March 11, 2019

Median Value of Family Net Worth

by Race or Ethnicity, 2016

White non-Hispanic	$171,000
Black or African-American	$17,150
Hispanic or Latino	$20,720
Other or Multiple Race	$64,620

$0 $25,000 $50,000 $75,000 $100,000 $125,000 $150,000 $175,000 $200,000

Source: The Federal Reserve Board, 2016 Survey of Consumer Finances (SCF), 2017

college-educated black woman account for much about me. Any attempt to erase these differences ultimately destabilizes us, because, despite our many connections, despite sitting across from each other, we have been pushed out of a structure from opposing ends through the doorway of our shared culture, to sit across from each other. I begin to remember all the turbulence and disturbances between us that contributed to the making of this moment of ease and comfort.

After my friend's departure, I pick up my mistake like a snow globe and turn it over in my mind. My assumption reminds me of a comment made by a white man on a flight I took: "I don't see color." Like him, a lack of discomfort allowed me, for a nanosecond, to disregard history and the institutional structures put in place to predetermine that my friend and I can never slip on sameness.

Was my slipup simply a misplaced desire to calcify our connection, or is there more? Was the slip an otherworldly desire to become my friend, take on the trappings of her white life, and form a semblance of equality that can never exist? I understand that my need even to ask this question is formulated within a white-centered framework that believes all aspirational life is toward whiteness. The framework of white hierarchy has been behind the making of a culture I am both subject to and within. Consequently, I know how easily my actions could be formed by it. Why not want the thing that offers the most lasting and stable, if at times toxic and dehumanizing, value?

The life I've made is my life, and though it overlaps with what's also desired by white people like my WASP friend—our houses, for example—there are agendas that build precariousness and trauma into any professional success I have achieved that must

remain more primary for me. An essential desire for equity and the ability to live freely without the fear of white terrorism literally trumps everything, as former first lady Michelle Obama expresses in *Becoming*.

Unless something structural shifts in ways that remain unimaginable, the life my friend has is not a life I can achieve. Ever. Her kind of security, because it's not merely monetary, is atmospheric and therefore is not transferable. It's what reigns invisible behind the term "white." It doesn't inoculate her from illness, loss, or forfeiture of wealth, but it ensures a level of citizenry, safety, mobility, and belonging I can never have. Neither of us is baffled by our particular, random, well-earned, unearned, historical, or inherited differences. It is in fact my friend's ability to grasp and hold our differences that creates both our facility with each other and our antagonisms. But why, even for a second, translate ease with each other into a state of sameness?

If no sameness of status is possible, even within my closest white friendships, how to account for closeness? What form of relation can include knowledge of historical dynamics and societal realities without preventing or interrupting intimacy? If similarity and sameness are essentially impossible, how is "difference" recouped and aligned with closeness? How do we keep all the differences on the table and still call that a friendship?

I long to trust in our feelings of closeness, a closeness years in the making that wrestled racism and racist assumptions to the surface of our hurt feelings and profound disappointments. I wish to stop time and have feelings of intimacy blanket all time, both historical time and the years that took us from our late twenties to our late fifties. But to stop being conscious of my friend's innate advantages is to stop being present inside our relationship.

Text *My friend already knows the truth of her life before I call it forward.*

Notes and Sources Dorothy A. Brown, "Shades of the American Dream," *Washington University Law Review*: "Whites are most likely to own their own homes (76%), followed by Asians (61%), Latinos (49%), and blacks (48%). Race matters when it comes to being a homeowner. Being white makes you significantly more likely to own a home than if you are Asian, black, or Latino. . . . Even though Asians are more likely to be homeowners than blacks and Latinos, given that Asian median income is higher than white median income, we might expect to see even higher homeownership rates for Asians than whites—yet we do not. . . . Homeownership disparities by race and ethnicity are not solely attributable to differences in income. Even at high income levels, a smaller percentage of blacks and Latinos are homeowners than whites. In 2005, for every income level, black homeownership rates were less than the overall homeownership rates by income."

To remember the truth of us is to be in the truth of us, in all its realities and all its stumbles and slips. Then our friendship is what allows us to fall away from the ease of intimacy without falling.

My friend already knows the truth of her life before I call it forward. Her ability not to push aside the moment of my self-correct, a moment that happens with language, language that seems to distance us from each other in its effort to know precisely, points to her ability to hold and recognize her advantages, her disadvantages, her whiteness, alongside my blackness, my disadvantages, and my advantages, despite our similarities.

The two-step, just us, no, you and I, that I enacted is one she, I hope, kept in step with. I doubt she would have corrected me had I not corrected myself, but that aside, together we allowed racial difference, as constructed as it is, as real as it is, not to become for us a source of acrimonious silence. Our fortitude, our resilience with regard to each other's differences becomes in day-to-day life our friendship.

Still, when I asked her to respond to an earlier version of this piece, she said she had no thoughts of interest. I keep wondering how she, a writer with a wealth of thoughts and imaginings, had suddenly gone bankrupt.

ethical loneliness

i

I go to see *Fairview*, a play by Jackie Sibblies Drury, with a white female friend. She's interested in thinking about whiteness; this play is interested in thinking about race. We are covered in all directions.

Near the end of the play, the fourth wall is broken. A character asks the white members of the audience to get up from their seats and walk on the stage, which has been transformed into a beige living and dining room with a staircase leading to the second floor. Faces will be revealed, composure tested. Effort must be made to stay within the requests of the play. The black actor wishes the space of the audience to hold black people in a way the world does not. The request is presented as a conditional—what if? What if the audience, in this space of the imagination, can enact something that doesn't exist in our world?

Is the stage now a segregated space as the black actors join the blacks in the audience? Has center stage transformed into the front of the bus? Or is it now a Whites Only boardroom? In the moment, no one knows what really is being proclaimed. A white man in the seat behind me says, This is fucked up. Nonetheless, he makes his way to the stage.

The white woman I am with remains in her seat. I am getting tense. The playwright is a black woman, and I am a black woman, and I want her play to have what it has requested. What I assume it needs. Is my identification with the playwright because she's black, or because she's a woman, or because she's an artist? It's impossible to dissect. My tension begins to couple with a building resentment against my white friend. I feel betrayed by her.

I am not the playwright. The playwright might think the success of the play depends on some white people staying in their seats.

From a June 1981 keynote presentation Audre Lorde gave at the National Women's Studies Association Conference, Storrs, Connecticut.

Women responding to racism means women responding to anger, the anger of exclusion, of unquestioned privilege, of racial distortions, of silence, ill-use, stereotyping, defensiveness, misnaming, betrayal, and coopting.

My anger is a response to racist attitudes, to the actions and presumptions that arise out of those attitudes. If in your dealings with other women your actions have reflected those attitudes, then my anger and your attendant fears, perhaps, are spotlights that can be used for your growth in the same way I have had to use learning to express anger for my growth. But for corrective surgery, not guilt. Guilt and defensiveness are bricks in a wall against which we will all perish, for they serve none of our futures.

The playwright might be waiting for a black person to get on the stage with the white people. None do. The playwright might want me to think her request is divisive and walk out of the theater: not a black stage, not a white stage, but a "United Stage." The playwright might have calculated what percentage of the audience, "white members of the audience," would not comply. Are my unbearable feelings a sign that I, a black member of the audience, remain inside the play? The playwright might think, Why are they listening to me? as more and more white audience members fill up the stage and people of color stay seated. Will the stage hold all the white people? Or, and this is what is troubling me, the playwright might have said exactly what she wants to happen.

I am trying to listen to the actor speak the closing lines of the play, which it turns out are composed of quotes from famous black writers, but all I can think about is my white friend's non-compliant presence in her seat. Why won't she do what was asked? I can't understand why she can't do such a simple thing. Why can't she see it matters? Does it matter? In the sense that race matters, her refusal feels like an insistence on full ownership of the entire theater. Oh, God. I am beginning to feel pushed out of my own seat for the last minutes of the play. Burdened by my association with her refusal, a moment of Fremdschämen perhaps.

Taxi.

I want to run. Away from what? An embodied refusal I can't help but see and one that surprises me? My own mounting emotion in the face of what I perceive as belligerence? A friendship error despite my understanding of how whiteness functions? I thought we shared the same worldview, if not the same privileges. Be still my beating, breaking heart?

Anger is loaded with information and energy. When I speak of women of Color, I do not only mean Black women. . . . The woman of Color who charges me with rendering her invisible by assuming that her struggles with racism are identical with my own has something to tell me that I had better learn from, lest we both waste ourselves fighting the truths between us. If I participate, knowingly or otherwise, in my sister's oppression and she calls me on it, to answer her anger with my own only blankets the substance of our exchange with reaction. It wastes energy I need to join her. And yes, it is very difficult to stand still and to listen to another woman's voice delineate an agony I do not share, or even one in which I myself may have participated.

When the play finally ends, I say to my confounding friend, I didn't know you were black.

She doesn't respond.

Given the irritation in my voice, it's not a comment seeking a response. It's my performance of my own refusal to engage beyond the terms of the play. Her performance of resistance felt like no solidarity, insofar as I, as a black person, dropped away as the request of the play dropped away. She must understand the play's request is made in response to a world where black people's requests don't matter. Why doesn't she recognize the moment as an offering of black Feminism?

Though my friend and I are in the habit of checking in every few days, over the next couple of weeks we speak of everything but this day. Still, I can't stop returning to the image of her glued to her seat. She was five rows from the stage. Why does the memory continue to infuriate and perplex me? Why am I not able to read this moment? Why am I not able to stop reading this moment? Why am I unable to settle it down and file it away?

I attempt to answer my silent questions by remembering my therapist once told me that some white patients who identify with trauma and victimization see themselves as black or Jewish in their dreams. Their understanding of what they have experienced, how they feel, becomes apprehensible only through the lens of antiblack racism or anti-Semitism. To fully embody their pain, their trauma, they need it to mirror historical, institutional structures that are defined by an incomprehensible event like slavery or the Holocaust. Their feelings of loneliness, stuckness, or stasis

And while we scrutinize the often painful face of each other's anger, please remember that it is not our anger which makes me caution you to lock your doors at night, and not to wander the streets of Hartford alone. It is the hatred which lurks in those streets, that urge to destroy us all if we truly work for change rather than merely indulge in our academic rhetoric.

This hatred and our anger are very different. Hatred is the fury of those who do not share our goals, and its object is death and destruction. Anger is the grief of distortions between peers, and its object is change. But our time is getting shorter. We have been raised to view any difference other than sex as a reason for destruction, and for Black women and white women to face each other's angers without denial or immobilization or silence or guilt is in itself a heretical and generative idea. It implies peers meeting upon a common basis to examine difference, and to alter those distortions which history has created around difference. For it is those distortions which separate us. And we must ask ourselves: Who profits from all this?

feel similar to, though different from, what the theorist Jill Stauffer describes as ethical loneliness. Her exact words are "Ethical loneliness is the isolation one feels when one, as a violated person or as one member of a persecuted group, has been abandoned by humanity, or by those who have power over one's life's possibilities."

Is my friend's refusal to move, to be seen moving, a move she needed to make? Is it a message, a performance of one? Is she telling the black audience, you all don't get to look at me. You don't get to see me as a white specimen. This is fucked up, the man behind me had said. The unconscious, as I understand it, can lose context or perspective. Maybe my friend cannot bear to be told what to do, and how that started and where it will end has little to do with her whiteness or everything to do with her whiteness. My perception of a blind spot around racial dynamics could lead to a larger discussion of white feminism and white entitlement. Maybe I am only responding to her whiteness because the play constructed a scene around our unshared racial positioning. Maybe my own line of reasoning is such a stretch that it'll snap back to hit me in the face. Nonetheless, an incoherent sting lingers. I can't let it go. I won't let it go. What do you care? I ask myself. And still I care about the architecture of my intimacy with this woman. From this moment forward how easily will the pronoun "we" slip from my lips?

I ask my friend, this white woman who speaks of understanding and empathizing with so much, Why didn't you go onto the stage? She looks at me. Is there a pause? Time seems to gather the space of the differences between us. She says, I didn't want to.

I'm still looking at her. What does she see in my face? You didn't want to? Is she speaking about exhaustion? Exhaustion I can

I have no creative use for guilt, yours or my own. Guilt is only another way of avoiding informed action, of buying time out of the pressing need to make clear choices, out of the approaching storm that can feed the earth as well as bend the trees. If I speak to you in anger, at least I have spoken to you; I have not put a gun to your head and shot you down in the street; I have not looked at your bleeding sister's body and asked, "What did she do to deserve it?" This was the reaction of two white women to Mary Church Terrell's telling of the lynching of a pregnant Black woman whose baby was then torn from her body. That was in 1921, and Alice Paul had just refused to publicly endorse the enforcement of the Nineteenth Amendment for all women—excluding the women of Color who had worked to help bring about that amendment.

understand. Exhaustion is tied to fatigue, and addressing the on-slaught of an eternally rejuvenating racism brings forward fatigue in all of us. Or, is this simply, I don't have to do what a black woman tells me to do. I am white. Can't you see that?

I didn't want to. And what I want is what matters. At the end, in the end, I am a white woman. I am the one who matters. I didn't want to. Are these the unspoken sentences that I am to defer to?

Within the little that I know of this woman, and this moment seems to show how little the little is, I know her answer to me is no answer. I know the real answer, or more realistically the real exploration, is within the conversations she has with other people, perhaps other white people, perhaps her white therapist. Those conversations in my imagination hold me as the one who cannot let anything go—anything like slavery, as if slavery hasn't morphed and adapted itself to our century through mass incar-ceration and institutional inequities—because of my own over-whelming sense of, of, of, yes, ethical loneliness. I am not her confidante. I am not to be shared with. I am not one—I am not the one she trusts with her whiteness. I am not, as I had thought, the friend I imagine.

These are the missteps, misunderstandings, and recognitions of friendships. After I write all this down, I share it with her because we are friends. I don't want it between us as either surprise or secret. I tell her its content is ours to deal with first. We are both learning how to move through our understandings together. She says the piece correctly narrates what she said and did, so she doesn't feel misrepresented. The thoughts are mine, but the ac-tions are indeed hers. Then she explains that she "felt harangued by the play along familiar lines. I didn't want to move. I didn't

The angers between women will not kill us if we can articulate them with precision, if we listen to the content of what is said with at least as much intensity as we defend ourselves from the manner of saying. . . . When we turn from anger we turn from insight, saying we will accept only the designs already known, those deadly and safely familiar. I have tried to learn my anger's usefulness to me, as well as its limitations.

want to be in this." Hers was a "frustrating and frustrated feeling, a sad feeling, also a taken-to-task-again feeling, all at once." She also felt the play was brilliant and doesn't wish the play to have done anything differently.

And then she did something I didn't expect but that explains why we are friends. She sat down and wrote.

So of course, post-talking to you, and aided by the gym's treadmill, my brain started popping more thoughts (part of why I so love talking to you). Only now getting a chance to put thoughts down.

Maybe of interest to you and important to me: I know I shrink, sometimes a lot, sometimes a little, from scenes where I'm asked, personally or generally, to feel bad as a white person—where, whatever else is being asked, I'm also being asked to feel shame, guilt, to do penance, to stand corrected, to sit down chastised. Obviously, some of this shrinking is just because—who wouldn't?—no one enjoys being chastised. Or do they? This is where my reaction becomes important to me: I react with a kind of nausea when I smell, as Darryl Pinckney put it, "White audiences [who] confuse having been chastised with learning" (in his NYRB piece about Afro-pessimism). Of course, there are reasons to feel shame, guilt, to be corrected, etc.— that is, there is real history, and there are real situations and experiences and exchanges that call for them, and some of my reaction is (per "who wouldn't?") straight-up defensive. But situations (claims, blogposts, diversity workshop activities, whatever) manufactured specifically to elicit white shame, penance, etc., make me uneasy—I feel like unholy transactions are in the offing, like white moral masochism is getting a thrill.

I think I've told you this story, but I remember, at a diversity workshop, a new colleague, a young white man, saying that the hardest thing about work on diversity, equity, and inclusion (the blank we were asked to fill in) was something like not letting the emotional challenges of the work, and the psychic toll of it, convince him that he had done something just by riding the white emotional roller-coaster. Is it too much of a rationalization to say that I didn't want to play along with the display of white shame and resolve at the end (much as I thought it was a brilliant way to end the play) because it felt like an enactment of just this?

Some of the frustration and exhaustion I felt in that moment had to do with how repetitive the calls for white people to look at ourselves, to step up, to

move off our comfortable asses, etc., are. That the calls were quotations (I think Hughes, Du Bois, Alain Locke, maybe Hurston) made perfect sad sense to me: I suspect some of my frustration, exhaustion, and sadness is that the calls get made, over and over and over, brilliantly and urgently, and so many white people shrug, or thrill to them emotionally but then do nothing.

Of course, in a way I was doing nothing by sitting, and there was no way from the outside to know what I was thinking—the easiest thought to attribute to me might have been "This is fucked up," and in a way, that is the right thought. I think that if other white people had not gotten up, or if it seemed like not enough were getting up, I would have. I wanted the play to work; I tend to feel responsible. I think I hoped my resisting the stage could somehow be a piece of a fully successful ending: not all the white people got up—interesting.

I loved the part in your piece about what a therapist told you about white people dreaming they are black or Jewish as a way of inhabiting pain. I'm sure I've told you that, as a child, I read, over and over, every book our local library had on the Holocaust, on US slavery, and also on witch trials and medieval torture devices—I needed scenes on which to hang my sense that people are unbelievably cruel to people close at hand. I didn't think I was black at the end of the play, but I was all over the place—so sick of white people, so identified with those who feel watched (the black people in the play), so in awe of the play, shaky. Claiming/owning whiteness, in that moment, by getting up, felt hard. I felt glued to my seat. I'm sure there is a lot more to say/think/analyze about all of this but that's the phenomenological truth of it, for fucked-up and otherwise.

I appreciated my friend's response even as I began to engage it critically. But, also, always there remains her life, her experieces that speak back to me. I am in my head and in my heart simultaneously. What I know is I can always ask, even as I'm feeling what I don't want to feel. I can always ask.

iii

                                        A charac-
ter asks the white members of the audience to get up

                                   The black actor
wishes the space   to hold black people
                                              —what
if

The white woman   remains in her seat.

              The playwright might think

An embodied refusal

                                                            still

She doesn't respond.

                                        refusal
                                                        like
                a   dropped

        dream

I didn't want to.

        no

cannot

                I am not
the   whiteness.
            I imagine.

liminal spaces ii

Text *In response to Kitt, it was reported that Lady Bird Johnson cried.*

Fact Check No. This may be true, but both sides allegedly later deny that she actually cried.

Notes and Sources According to a *USA Today* report titled "Eartha Kitt's Vietnam Comments Nearly Ended Her Career," Lady Bird Johnson wrote in a private diary that "one paper said that I was pale and that my voice trembled slightly as I replied to Miss Kitt. I think that is correct. I did not have tears in my eyes as another paper said." Kitt's daughter told the paper that "my mother said she never saw tears."

What does it mean to re-create conversations in detail in order to unmask—what? The self-positioned? The self in relation to another, an other?

What lives in the encounter? What's in the openness of that? Is the important thing what's said or what goes unsaid? Is the moment the moment before the words are shared or the moment after?

To live only in the archives of conversations is, perhaps, to see what the culture has formed, willingly. Repeatedly? Sure.

> President Lyndon B. Johnson, who signed the Civil Rights Act in 1964, said to Bill Moyers: *If you can convince the lowest white man he's better than the best colored man, he won't notice you're picking his pocket. Hell, give him somebody to look down on, and he'll empty his pockets for you.*

> Eartha Kitt at a 1968 White House luncheon, said to Lady Bird Johnson: *You send the best of this country off to a war and they get shot and maimed. They don't want that. . . . They rebel in the streets, they will take pot. If you don't know the expression, it is marijuana.*

> In response to Kitt, it was reported that Lady Bird Johnson cried in case anyone failed to hear the harm inflicted by Kitt's comment. The CIA created a dossier on Kitt a week after the luncheon. She was then blacklisted in the United States for the next decade.

To converse is to risk the unraveling of the said and the unsaid.

To converse is to risk the performance of what's held by the silence.

Thomas Jefferson in *Notes on the State of Virginia*:

It will probably be asked, Why not retain and incorporate the blacks into the state, and thus save the expence of supplying, by importation of white settlers, the vacancies they will leave? Deep rooted prejudices entertained by the whites; ten thousand recollections, by the blacks, of the injuries they have sustained; new provocations; the real distinctions which nature has made; and many other circumstances, will divide us into parties, and produce convulsions which will probably never end but in the extermination of the one or the other race.—To these objections, which are political, may be added others, which are physical and moral. The first difference which strikes us is that of colour. Whether the black of the negro resides in the reticular membrane between the skin and scarf-skin, or in the scarf-skin itself; whether it proceeds from the colour of the blood, the colour of the bile, or from that of some other secretion, the difference is fixed in nature, and is as real as if its seat and cause were better known to us. And is this difference of no importance?

What is wanted? What is being said, what is being shared, what is being known for all time?

Starbucks employee to 911 operator: *Hi, I have two gentlemen at my café that are refusing to make a purchase or leave. I'm at the Starbucks at 18th and Spruce.*

What is the "never" at the center of the moment, what is the "never again," what is the "not," the "no" in the utterance?

Are conversations desire projected? Is conversing a dance? The back-and-forth, a chance? To take? Or be taken? To be taken away? Taken out?

What is being threatened? What is being defended? What is being taken away? Is everything being taken away? What is it?

What is offended? Offensive? Is it simply because I am? Or, because you are? Am I in your way? That you step in my way? Do I know you? Can I know you? In your ways? Anyways?

> HILARY BROOKE MUELLER: *You can film me. That's fine—*
> D'ARREION TOLES: *I understand, ma'am, but you're blocking me.*
> MUELLER: *Into my building.*
> TOLES: *OK, and it's my building as well, so I need you to get out my way and—*
> MUELLER: *OK, what unit?*
> TOLES: *I don't need to say that information, so 'scuse me, ma'am.*
> MUELLER: *I'm uncomfortable.*
> TOLES: *Excuse me. OK, you can be uncomfortable, that's your discretion. You're uncomfortable 'cause of you. I need you to move out of my way, please.*
> MUELLER: *No.*

Just us, just people, the same people, but what is it that the just people are feeling or wanting or being? The brouhaha so brutal, rising, rising up, rise up.

What rises up within, between us? What comes up because we are the history within us?

911 OPERATOR: *San Francisco 911. What's the exact location of your emergency?*
ALISON ETTEL: *I'm on the sidewalk. Hi. I'm having someone that does not have a vendor permit that's selling water across from the ballpark.*
OPERATOR: *Uhhh . . .*
ETTEL: *Do you have someone I can talk to about that?*
OPERATOR: *Okay, one second. Let me transfer you over to the police department. Hang on.*
ETTEL: *Great, thank you.*
ETTEL: *Hi. I'm having someone that, um, does not have a vendor permit that's selling water across from the ballpark.*

What is the incoherence that calls? What calls by name, what makes the feeling rage? What makes the feeling the sureness of ignorance, the blindness of frost? The lawlessness of loss?

Unidentified white woman: *It don't bother me if I say it and I don't care if everybody hears me. I think everybody here feels the same way I do, Go back to wherever the fuck you come from, lady.*

A force within the whiteness is forcing the whiteness.

What is the feeling that pulls, that is pulling, that pulls it out, what sensation uncivilized the utterance? What? What dragged us, just us, here? What is the justice wanted?

Then the black person is asked to leave to vacate to prove to validate to confirm to authorize to legalize their right to be in the air in air

Text *. . . the police help help is called help help the police is called the police help help.*

Notes and Sources Zak Cheney-Rice, "NYPD Union Lawyers Argue That Eric Garner Would've Died Anyway Because He Was Obese," *New York* magazine: "Pantaleo's defense team has claimed consistently that Garner was responsible for his own death. Were he not overweight and asthmatic, they argue, he would have survived the violence to which he was subjected. While it may seem odd to suggest that a victim's physical health should be used to exonerate someone who choked and killed him, it is consistent with the logic applied to many cases where police skate for killing unarmed civilians—many of which hinge on how the victims might have prevented themselves from dying in the first place, whether by maintaining better physical fitness in Garner's case, or appearing less scary to police, as in the cases of Michael Brown, Terence Crutcher, and others."

in here and then the police help help is called help help the police ● is called the police help help.

More often than not the police back up support reinforce the claims of the person who calls called them in the whiteness of truth the whiteness of victimhood in the whitening benefit of the doubt in the whiter–than–white explanation of.

EARL:	*They're not loitering.*
JM:	*How am I loitering in an area that's public?*
EARL:	*You're sitting here.*
JM:	*So this area is off limits after a certain time?*
EARL:	*Only if you are a guest.*
JM:	*I am a guest.*
EARL:	*You didn't tell me that.*
JM:	*I said that I am a guest I told you that.*
EARL:	*I asked what room you are in you refused.*
JM:	*I am in 5 something I just checked in today, here's my ticket, my uh, room, just checked in with my American Express and these gentlemen are harassing me.*
LOUIS:	*No one is harassing you man.*
JM:	*You are.*
LOUIS:	*I am just trying to get to the bottom of it.*
JM:	*There is nothing to get to the bottom of, sir. Do you want to check and see if I am a guest?*

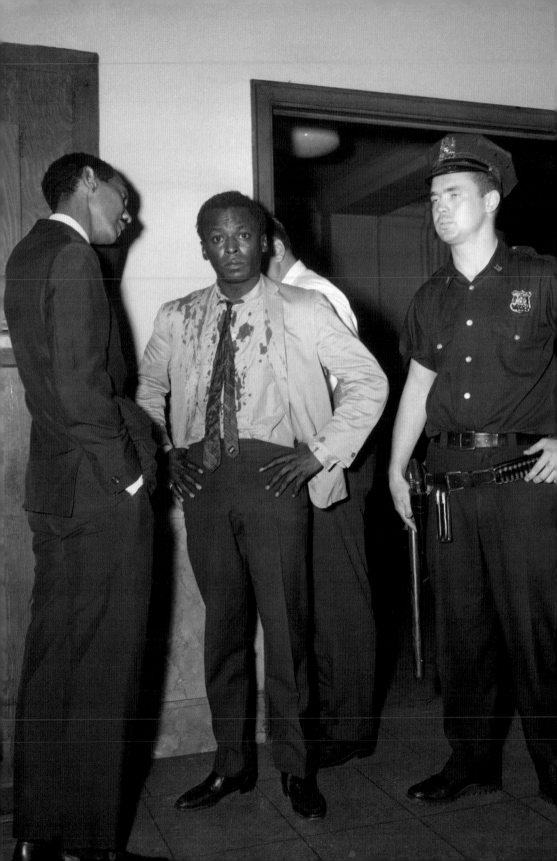

LOUIS:	*That's why I ask you, man. I'm trying to help you out here, bro.*
JM:	*No, I'll like to see the cops. Let the cops come, please.*
LOUIS:	*That's fine. All right.*
EARL:	*See what I am dealing with.*
JM:	*You guys are crazy*
	. . .
JM:	*Because Earl told me I need to leave?*
POLICE:	*Earl is in control of the property, yeah.*
JM:	*So Earl runs this place . . .*
POLICE:	*He does right now.*
JM:	*I am sitting here taking a phone call . . .*
POLICE:	*You can narrate this . . .*

The police they believe the police believe the president the history the education the media what entertainment taught them the world they know the worst they carry.

That's how we know this is not a mental health issue. This is not an isolated issue. This is not deserving of or serving us.

josé martí

Text *Brooklyn. She worries that her son will be killed. Killed by whom? My fantasy or her fantasy? Have you been to Brooklyn lately?*

Notes and Sources Crime rates in general in New York City are at the lowest levels in decades—see coverage from the *New York Times*: "Crime in New York City Plunges to a Level Not Seen Since the 1950s." There has been a slight uptick in Brooklyn very recently but in the broader picture the numbers are still low. The *New York Times* on the recent situation in Brooklyn: "There have been 21 killings so far in the Brooklyn North precincts, compared to 12 at this time last year [2018]. Many of those killings have been clustered in neighborhoods like East New York and Brownsville. Others have occurred on the edges of rapidly gentrifying areas like Bushwick and Bedford-Stuyvesant, where there were four murders within a five-block radius earlier this year," but "the violence in Brooklyn is still a far cry from the crest of the murder wave of the early 1990s. By April in 1993, for instance, the same 10 precincts in Brooklyn North already had more than 80 killings." There is a significant racial disparity in crime victimization in New York, in that whites are killed and accosted at a lower rate than other groups. See the *Wall Street Journal* coverage of that aspect of the situation.

An NYC-wide report from the NYPD breaks down the race of crime victims. These are the most recent data available and refer to 2018. Key highlights (there are more categories available, and note also that "suspect" may have a specific meaning in this context): Murder: "Murder and Non-Negligent Manslaughter victims are most frequently Black (62.6%) or Hispanic (24.9%). White victims account for (9.6%) of all Murder and Non-Negligent Manslaughter victims while Asian/Pacific Islanders account for (2.8%) of all Murder and Non-Negligent Manslaughter victims. The race/ethnicity of known Murder and Non-Negligent Manslaughter suspects mirrors the victim population with Black (61.9%) and Hispanic (31.0%) suspects accounting for the majority of suspects. White suspects account for (5.4%) of all Murder and Non-Negligent Manslaughter suspects while Asian/ Pacific Islanders accounted for (1.7%) of the known Murder and Non-Negligent Manslaughter suspects." Robbery: "Robbery victims are most frequently Hispanic (38.7%) or Black (30.6%). Asian/Pacific Islander victims account for (15.8%) of all Robbery victims while Whites account for (13.9%) of all Robbery victims. The race/ethnicity of known Robbery suspects is primarily Black (65.8%). Hispanic suspects account for an additional (27.1%) of the suspect population. White suspects account for (4.6%) of all Robbery suspects while Asian/Pacific Islanders accounted for (2.4%) of known Robbery suspects."

An older white man tells the table his son will be shipping out again soon. He believes in the importance of military service, but that doesn't stop him from being anxious about his son's life. The white, female judge sitting next to me sympathizes with his position. She knows how he feels. Her son is moving to Brooklyn. Brooklyn? I sit quietly thinking of all the euphemisms whites use to pull forward white people's fantasy of black content, or is it my fantasy of their fantasy? Disagreeable content. Dangerous content. Fearful content. Brooklyn. She worries that her son will be killed. Killed by whom? My fantasy or her fantasy? Have you   ●
been to Brooklyn lately?

Why doesn't the judge say what she means? I'm aware I am struggling to stay silent at this moment. Do I engage the racism she might believe justified? Does she know a white person like her son who was murdered or robbed or even harmed in Brooklyn? Did she sentence enough Brooklynites to cement an equation between Brooklyn and war zone? Is my fantasy of her framed mostly by what I know about the justice system? Have I read *The New Jim Crow* too many times? Have I followed Bryan Stevenson's career too closely? Am I making a leap that doesn't exist? She implied Brooklyn might kill her son; she didn't say black, she didn't say Caribbean, she didn't say Latinx. What other communities do I know in Brooklyn? The Hasidic Jewish community? The Eastern Europeans? The Dominicans? The Koreans? Who is not living there? How sure can I be of what she meant? No one else at the table laughs at her statement. Am I projecting onto her without merit? Should I ask her if she fears her son will be killed by another gentrifying white male since most victims and suspects are neighbors?

How far away can I get from confrontation by using the language of inquiry? Where are you going with this analogy? Where have we landed with this comparison that is no comparison, Judge?

BLACK LIVES

Because I know, had 2016 gone differently, this white, female judge could now hold a position in our government, and we would all think that was better than what we received at the time, and it would seem better than what we got, I am falling forward into my own deep awareness of how hopelessly white and seemingly racist our hope remains. Am I wrong? Brooklyn, not black.

And whatever she meant, she is not the exception. Senator Bernie Sanders, who was the hope of so many, considering Democratic losses after the 2018 midterm elections, remarked, "There are a lot of white folks out there who are not necessarily racist who felt uncomfortable for the first time in their lives about whether or not they wanted to vote for an African-American." How is not voting for someone simply because they're black not racist? Though Sanders was not shy in labeling Brian Kemp's and Ron DeSantis's campaigns racist (in his own tweet, he said, "One ad the Republicans put out was even rejected by Fox television because of its racist content. . . . In Florida, Andrew Gillum, whom I was proud to stand with even during the primaries, faced week after week of racism from his opponent and allied forces. That's just a fact. And in the end, I believe those craven attacks founded in 'fear of the other' had an impact on the outcome. Stacey Abrams faced similar attacks, in addition to unprecedented voter suppression. That's a reality that has to change"), even he appeared to stop short when it came to labeling potential white voters as racist.

How can white Democratic and Independent candidates have black people's humanity in mind on a policy level when they themselves exhibit or condone racism with whatever apologetic language comes to mind? A 2019 example would be Joe Biden's invocation of two white segregationists as an example of his ability to work across the aisle.

Text *It's no wonder that in the race to whiteness certain Asians and Latinx and black people have been, in my fantasy of them, breathless to distance themselves from blackness.*

Fact Check Maybe. The broader context might complicate this claim. See examples below.

Notes and Sources Ellen D. Wu's widely cited history, *The Color of Success: Asian Americans and the Origins of the Model Minority*, argues that the Asian American assimilation is best understood as a process inseparable from a white supremacist social structure rather than a product of Asian American desire alone: "Before the 1940s and 1950s, whites had deemed ethnic Japanese and Chinese unassimilable aliens unfit for membership in the nation. Americans had subjected so-called Orientals to the regime of Asiatic Exclusion, marking them as *definitively not-white*, and systematically shutting them out of civic participation through such measures as bars to naturalization, occupational discrimination, and residential segregation. Beginning in World War II, however, the United States' geopolitical ambitions triggered seismic changes in popular notions of nationhood and belonging. . . . By the mid-1960s . . . a new stereotype of Asian Americans as the model minority [had been invented]—a racial group distinct from the white majority, but lauded as well assimilated, upwardly mobile, politically nonthreatening, and *definitively not-black*." See also her *Washington Post* interview: "The model minority myth as we see it today was mainly an unintended outcome of earlier attempts by Asian Americans to be accepted and recognized as human beings."

A 2016 Pew Research study, *How U.S. Afro-Latinos Report Their Race*, found that only 18 percent of self-identified Afro-Latinos also identify as black.

See also Allyson Hobbs's book *The Chosen Exile*: *A History of Racial Passing in American Life*.

I know that "simply to be white is to be racist" is the catchphrase some liberals use these days, but when will they begin hearing what supposedly they know? When will knowledge matter to practice? "The landscape of your word is the world's landscape," wrote the Martinican writer, poet, and philosopher Édouard Glissant.

It's no wonder that in the race to whiteness certain Asian and Latinx and black people have been, in my fantasy of them, breathless to distance themselves from blackness. Claire Jean Kim argues that this is intentionally constructed by whites in her article "The Racial Triangulation of Asian Americans": "Racial triangulation occurs by means of two types of simultaneous, linked processes: (1) processes of 'relative valorization,' whereby dominant group A (Whites) valorizes subordinate group B (Asian Americans) relative to subordinate group C (Blacks) on cultural and/or racial grounds in order to dominate both groups, but especially the latter, and (2) processes of 'civic ostracism,' whereby dominant group A (Whites) constructs subordinate group B (Asian Americans) as immutably foreign and assimilable with Whites on cultural and/or racial grounds in order to ostracize them from the body politic and civic membership." This model in any case would be specific to Asian Americans and does not apply in the same way to our Latinx population.

But to return to our systems of government, an ineffective justice system points to deep-seated antiblack racism across the branches of our government. This is not disrupted because we have senators of color. Ted Cruz, formerly known as Rafael Edward Cruz, who is Irish-Cuban American, is my case in point of an unreliable anti-racist at a dinner party of mostly black and brown people. An artist at the party says Cruz doesn't represent her or Latinx people. She points out that there are many black-identified Latinx people whose views aren't represented anywhere in our discussion, not that being identified as black determines anything.

Text *Though assimilation into whiteness is very possible for some who identify as Latinx, many who self-identify as white are not treated or seen as white.*

Notes and Sources In her book *Race Migrations: Latinos and the Cultural Transformation of Race*, Wendy Roth analyzes the ways Puerto Rican and Dominican migrants assimilate into the US racial social structure based on their skin color. She argues, "The racial strategies that these migrants adopt—assimilation, code switching, and situational passing—are ultimately private solutions for dealing with racial barriers. They allow some light-skinned Puerto Ricans and Dominicans to step across the color line either momentarily or permanently, but they leave that color line in place behind them. Those with medium and dark skin are unable to cross into Whiteness, even momentarily. While adopting the cultural behavior of the dominant White group may improve their socioeconomic opportunities, they remain racialized as Latinos—a classification that brings some advantages in terms of affirmative-action considerations, but also many barriers. The private solutions associated with racial strategies may be helpful to some individuals, but public solutions are what break down racial barriers for all."

Text *Indigenous communities from places such as Mexico and the Central American countries are hardly accounted for.*

Notes and Sources The United States census forces those with Latinx indigenous identity into a race/ethnicity framework that is not necessarily relevant to their lived experience. A *New York Times* article, "Hispanics Identifying Themselves as Indians," by Geoffrey Decker, although dated, gives a good overview of the constraints that Latinx of indigenous origin face when filling out the American census form: "The American Indian totals are still a small fraction of the overall Hispanic population of the United States, which eclipsed 50 million this year. But the blip in the census data represents raised awareness among native Latinos who believe their heritage stretches farther back than the nationalities available on the census form."

Later, the artist sends everyone who attended the party a video link to a presentation by Miriam Jiménez Román, who makes the point that the census manipulates the Latinx population into racial identities because of its predetermined racial categories. "Latinx" is the gender-neutral term that replaces the previously used "Latino" and "Latina." Jiménez Román also points out that statistically a high percentage of Puerto Ricans in Puerto Rico identify as white. Though assimilation into whiteness is very possible for some who identify as Latinx, many who self-identify as white are not treated or seen as white. And those who self-identify as Afro-Latinx are ignored by blacks and erased by whites. Indigenous communities from places such as Mexico and the Central American countries are hardly accounted for.

Sitting at home replaying our conversation in my head, I consider calling the artist to continue our dinner-party conversation. The rain blurs the trees beyond my windows, and I wonder if this woman is as appalled by my ignorance as I sometimes feel in the company of whites. In some ways, I understand her to be the kind of interlocutor whom I need to engage, I want to engage. Alongside her willingness to challenge, I imagine there exists the desire to know and be known. I understand she'll ask for accountability in ways not meant to obfuscate but rather clarify. The clarity she demands makes apparent my own blind spots. I decide to call her.

On the phone she reiterates that she believes the Latinx assimilationist narrative is one constructed by whiteness itself. There's pressure for Latinx people to assimilate, she says. The pressure begins inside the national census, in the limits of its categories. The culture, when it talks about black excellence, rarely if ever includes examples of black Latinx. No one talks about the interchange of

Text *With only 18 percent of Afro-Latinx people identifying as black, many Latinx don't see themselves in either American whiteness or American blackness because they have cultures with specific histories and historical figures who aren't included in the American narrative.*

Notes and Sources See Pew data below.

See also "Socially Desirable Reporting and the Expression of Biological Concepts of Race" by Ann Morning, Hanna Brückner, and Alondra Nelson, *Du Bois Review: Social Science Research on Race.*

FEBRUARY 29, 2016

AFRO-LATINO: A DEEPLY ROOTED IDENTITY AMONG U.S. HISPANICS

How U.S. Afro-Latinos report their race

How U.S. Afro-Latinos report their race

White	39%
Hispanic (vol.)	24
Black	18
Mixed (2+ races, vol.)	9
American Indian (vol.)	4

Note: Races are based on any mentions of Hispanic, white, black, Asian, and American Indian as single race or multiple-race responses and are not mutually exclusive. "Mixed race" includes those who volunteered that they were "mixed race" or gave any two responses (including "Some other race" without specifying which race or volunteering "Hispanic" or "Latino" or a Hispanic origin as their race. Other races and "Don't know/Refused" are not shown. Source: National Survey of Latinos, conducted Sept. 11-Oct. 9, 2014 (N=1,520 Hispanic adults)

PEW RESEARCH CENTER

culture between African Americans and Afro-Cubans in the development of jazz, for example, she says. With only 18 percent of Afro-Latinx people identifying as black, many Latinx don't see themselves in either American whiteness or American blackness because they have cultures with specific histories and historical figures who aren't included in the American narrative.

I tell her I had a conversation with a Puerto Rican American man that I found amusing because I kept saying as "people of color" we need to organize around DACA, border issues, and proposed new immigration policies, and he kept saying as a "white man" he feels helpless under the current administration.

Ironically, "people of color" came from the term "women of color," which black women activists used as a term of solidarity with other non-white women until it eventually represented anyone who was not white identified. But people of color to him means black, she points out.

For me, people of color means "not structurally white," as in not a part of the structural power across institutions that want others dead or disenfranchised or deported or made invisible to white lives through voter suppression or passive or aggressive legislative defunding and criminalizing of certain segments of the population based both on race and ethnicity. But if, for example, as Jiménez Román said, 75.8 percent of Puerto Ricans in Puerto Rico see themselves as white and as part of the general group of white people, even as others don't see them that way, I see our conundrum.

My new friend, the artist, asks me, Did you know the Smithsonian, until its *Our America: The Latino Presence in American Art* exhibit in 2013, had never done a major show focused on the work of Latinos? No, I didn't know that.

Chris Rock

There ain't a white man in this room that would change places with me, none of you, none of you would change places with me and I'm rich.

What do you know about José Martí? Very little. He's a poet.

He's more than a poet. He's a poet is all anybody knows. OK.

Have you read *Harvest of Empire: A History of Latinos in America*? No.

So even as I understand the American stereotypes of Latinx people as gardeners and nannies to be intentionally devaluing, I also need to understand that our national cultural imagination, made up of celebrities and politicians (Sonia Sotomayor, Ted Cruz, Marco Rubio, J.Lo, and all the artists, writers, journalists, and other public figures in the mainstream), isn't an appropriate representation of the Latinx population at every level of American society, and with roots in countries all over the Americas and the Caribbean.

Sometimes in our conversation I forget to say Latinx, and use the term Latino or Hispanic when I want to refer to people of the Americas or Cubans like Cruz and Rubio, who have referred to themselves as Hispanics. This manages to bring our conversation to a halt. Hispanic is a racist term, the artist tells me. It refers back to Spain, serving to insert a European hierarchical lineage. I am reminded of dinner-party conversations when Jews heatedly distance themselves from those who cling to the label of German Jews. OK, I say, as I understand it's important what you call people, since Latinx is an ethnic identity, not a racial one.

I am becoming contrite, given my apparent monolithic focus on black-white relations in the United States, even though I believe antiblack racism is foundational to all of our problems, regardless of our ethnicity. It's this disconnect that keeps me saying the wrong thing. But I still have questions, and the way to get answers is to bear her corrections. I slow down so as not to make the same

Louis C.K.

I'm a lucky guy. I have a lot going for me. I'm healthy.
I'm relatively young. I'm white, which, thank god for
that shit boy. That's a huge leg up. Are you kidding
me? Oh, God, I love being white. I really do. Seriously,
if you're not white, you're missing out, because this
shit is thoroughly good. Let me be clear, by the way,
I am not saying that white people are better, I'm
saying being white is clearly better. Who could even
argue? If it was an option, I would re-up every year.
Oh, yeah, I'll take white again. I've been enjoying
that. I will stick with white, thank you.

James Patrick Connolly

In the year 2050, white people will no longer be the
majority in America; in LA that is so 2005.

But I grew up with diversity. I mean, I actually happen to
be half Mexican myself. OK, good idea, take your time,
stare at me as long as you need to. I know, nothing
screams Latino like James Patrick Connolly. . . .

There's a reason why I don't get up here and joke
about being white. And I feel very strongly about
this, because I think that white people have suffered
enough in this country already. We used to win golf
tournaments and the hundred-yard dash. There was a
time when a little white boy thought he might grow
up and be president of the United States someday.

mistakes. If I am to get things wrong, I want them to be different from before. A part of me wonders if white-identifying Latinx in power (is this an oxymoron?) aren't in collusion with the white establishment to distance Americans from the particularities of the ethnicities of various Latinx? Am I being defensive, or is this a fair question? Are intersectional alliances with a segment of the population that is often multiracial and that assimilates quickly through interracial marriage really possible? I remember my own surprise when I learned the infamous Louis C.K. was of Irish, Mexican, and Hungarian Jewish descent. While exposing some things, he seemed reticent to expose others. His multiracial identity isn't a recurring part of his routine, unlike fellow comedian James Patrick Connolly, who is also part Mexican.

I wonder if my new friend sees our developing friendship as a burden, given that, to share herself, she has to give me the tools to know her. How do I account for my own ignorance?

On the one hand, I have a friend who, as an Afro-Pessimist, argues that Latinx and Asian people are the "junior partners" in a white nationalist administration, and on the other, I know true solidarity has personally been an oversight on my part as my gaze has been focused on the dead and targeted black people unable just to live, though this limited and targeted existence is also true for many Latinx people.

I know these things, but it's phrases like "If he invited me to a public hanging, I'd be on the front row," stated by US senator Cindy Hyde-Smith of Mississippi while campaigning in a run-off election against Democratic challenger and African American Mike Espy, and Laura Ingraham's "shut up and dribble" targeted at LeBron James, and, and, and, that come to mind as I try to

EQUAL RIGHTS

LIBERTY UNDER THE LAW   TRUE INDUSTRIAL FREEDOM

Los Angeles Times

WEDNESDAY MORNING, FEBRUARY 20, 1946

RULING GIVES MEXICAN CHILDREN EQUAL RIGHTS

Segregation of Mexican schoolchildren from others in f o u r Santa Ana school districts yesterday was held by U.S. Judge Paul J. McCormick to be a violation of their guarantees of equal rights under the 14th Amendment of the Constitution. The opinion was written in

tion of the State. He held that inasmuch as violations of the 14th Amendment were indicated, the Federal court had a right to intervene.

"The evidence clearly shows," the opinion states, "that Spanish-speaking children are retarded in learning English by lack of exposure to its use because

"All the News That's Fit to Print"

The New York Times.

LATE CITY EDITION
Fair and cool today. Mostly sunny, continued cool tomorrow.

VOL. CIII...No. 35,178.   NEW YORK, TUESDAY, MAY 18, 1954.   FIVE CENTS

HIGH COURT BANS SCHOOL SEGREGATION; 9-TO-0 DECISION GRANTS TIME TO COMPLY

McCarthy Hearing Off a Week as Eisenhower Bars Report

SENATOR IS IRATE

President Orders Aides Not to Disclose Details of Top-Level Meeting

Communist Arms Unloaded in Guatemala By Vessel From Polish Port, U. S. Learns

State Department Views News Gravely Because of Red Infiltration

REACTION OF SOUTH

'Breathing Spell' for Adjustment Tempers Region's Feelings

1896 RULING UPSET

'Separate but Equal' Doctrine Held Out of Place in Education

SOVIET BIDS VIENNA CEASE 'INTRIGUES'

City Colleges' Board Can't Pick Chairman

2 TAX PROJECTS DIE IN ESTIMATE BOARD

meet this friend where she stands. Maybe I should be thinking about ICE, or threats of repealing DACA, or concentration camps passing themselves off as detention centers, or "shithole countries" comments, or historical moments like the lynchings of Mexicans by white supremacist mobs in California or the constant humiliations and the intense psychic damage that would lead someone like Sammy Sosa to lighten his skin: "It's a bleaching cream that I apply before going to bed and [it] whitens my skin some." It's hard to separate his words from our culture's deep hatred of blackness.

Do I honestly feel the same level of distress toward Latinx people as I do toward white people given that all people of color live under the thumb of white supremacy and legislative power remains predominantly in the hands of white people? Obviously not, but . . .

I hear both exasperation and patience in my new friend's voice as I say all this. She reminds me no one said much of anything when the president called Mexicans rapists. I beg to differ as to private conversations, but in the public writing I do, I can't argue. Later she reminds me of the growing population of Latinx communities in the United States, a claim supported by Antonio Flores. His Pew report, "How the U.S. Hispanic Population Is Changing," states that "the Latino population in the United States has reached nearly 58 million in 2016 and has been the principal driver of U.S. demographic growth, accounting for half of national population growth since 2000. . . . In 2016, Hispanics accounted for 18% of the nation's population and were the second-largest racial or ethnic group behind whites. . . . They are also the nation's second-fastest-growing racial or ethnic group, with a 2.0% growth rate between 2015 and 2016 compared with a 3.0% rate for Asians."

Also, Obama's 2008 presidential campaign slogan Yes, We Can! finds its roots in ¡Sí Se Puede!, the trademarked motto of the

SÍ SE PUEDE!

Notes and Sources Elizabeth Martínez, in discussion with Angela Y. Davis, "Coalition Building among People of Color," University of California–Santa Cruz Center for Cultural Studies: "There are various forms of working together. A coalition is one, a network is another, an alliance is yet another. And they are not the same; some of them are short-term, and some are long-term. A network is not the same as a coalition. A network is a more permanent, ongoing thing. I think you have to look at what the demands are, and ask: What kind of coming together do we need to win these demands? And if you know the administration will pick your groups off one by one, then the largest umbrella you can possibly get is probably the best one. Some of the answers to your question are tactical and depend upon the circumstances. But the general idea is no competition of hierarchies should prevail. No 'Oppression Olympics'!"

YES WE CAN!

United Farm Workers of America, founded by Cesar Chavez, ●
Dolores Huerta, Gilbert Padilla, Larry Itliong, and Philip Vera
Cruz—a fact Obama no doubt calculated and a voting bloc he
surely depended on in his intersectional campaign strategies.

Nonetheless, what the artist and I want, whether or not we agree,
has little to do with our individual persons and everything to do
with our longings for our life possibilities.

I send what I have written to yet another friend who is multi-
racial. She asks if I have read Wendy Trevino's *Brazilian Is Not a
Race*. Yes, I say, as I quote her lines: "We are who we are / To
them, even when we don't know who we / Are to each other &
culture is a / Record of us figuring that out." This other friend, a
Mexican and Persian Muslim woman, doesn't see herself so much
in the conversation I've had with the artist. She says:

*So after reading your conversation with this artist, I find myself thinking
about my own positionality, as a woman of color who is not black and who
studies black culture. I am also thinking about the conversations that I have
had with other graduate students in my department. Some of these people
are white, some are black, and some are interracial like me. These conver-
sations can be so fraught even in academic communities when talking about
what also happens to us (who is us? what us?), without being caught up
in what we understand to be "oppression olympics."*

*I think about the many conversations I have had with a friend who like me
is a Muslim of color who is not black and who studies black history, and
our own experiences with prejudice and racism—how do those experiences
fit in the work that we do? In a very deep way those experiences have
brought us to our work—there is an obligation we feel to that work that is
about what this country we are in is predicated on.*

One thing we have talked about is the number of times Islamophobia has taken us so off-guard—including among those in our field, who are black and otherwise. Sometimes this happens when people do not realize exactly who we are, and it always feels like a disappointment. I don't know what to do with this feeling, or how to always talk about it openly without sounding like I am playing oppression olympics—I get anxious because this is not what I want to do, and do not always know to what degree I should expect a reciprocation of understanding. Or: to what degree I should be as patient as I try to be.

I do think there is an extent to which our Americanness makes it possible for us to think about these things as though they are abstractions. To people in other countries, at the end of the day, to be an American citizen means yup *such an immense privilege.*

When I wake in the middle of the night, I sit at my desk and my friend's phrase "reciprocation of understanding" comes back to me. Is that what we are after? Are conversations pathways to the exchange of understandings? When I am on my own in the dark, the stakes seem lower and perhaps more achievable than say something like "entangled empathy," which a philosopher friend of mine argues for. For her entangled empathy is not a feeling but a perspective where you recognize yourself inside a complicated set of relations. But what happens when "reciprocate" is a command. I have understood, therefore you must. The defensiveness that brings forward is only human, but is there a moment or a sentence after any reaction of vulnerability that would give us time to realign? Maybe our social work becomes our attempt to be in relation. Conversations could be redefined as such.

What does it mean to want a thing to change but then feel bullied by that change? Is understanding change? I am not sure.

The playwright and poet Samuel Beckett once said that writing ●
Waiting for Godot was a way of finding "a form that accommodates the mess." Are conversations accommodations?

Perhaps words are like rooms; they have to make room for people. Dude, I am here. We are here.

You are here. She is here. They are here. He is here. We live here too. He eats here too. She walks here too. He waits here too. They shop here too. Dude! Come on. Come on.

boys will be boys

Text *They're both white and the woman is out of a Ralph Lauren ad: dyed blond hair, Gucci loafers, capri pants, a sweater set. The clothes are meant to signal race through class. We have seen versions of this woman many times before even as the "timeless" appears dated. The man is over six feet tall and well groomed in khakis . . .*

Notes and Sources Tom Reichert and Tray LaCaze analyzed 237 Ralph Lauren ads in *GQ* from January 1980 to December 2000, coding them as "country club" if they depicted "scenes and models that exhibited an association with wealth, influence, and luxury featuring models shown in upscale dress or clean-cut appearances participating or observing polo, yachting, sailing, equestrian activities, and formal functions." There is ample evidence that Ralph Lauren's class politics were central to the brand in its conception (see also *Ralph Lauren*, a book-length history in Lauren's own words). Classic advertisements that speak to Ralph Lauren's role in shaping the image of upper-class style in the United States include the advertisements for a nouveau riche revival of the Hamptons in the 1980s and an ad campaign for the scent "Safari" set in what one author calls vaguely imperial settings.

From G. Bruce Boyer's 1987 *New York Times* article, "Khaki": "Outside of India, the first troops officially to adopt khaki (from the Hindi word khak, meaning 'dust-colored') were the 74th Foot, a Scottish regiment that wore khaki tunics with their tartan trousers during the South African Kaffir War (1851–53). . . . Khaki also owes its civilian uses to soldiers: After World War II, veterans returning to college brought their khakis to campus. . . . Combined with penny loafers, an oxford button-down shirt and a crew-neck sweater, khakis achieved a certain style. . . . By the advent of the Ivy League styles of the 1950's, khaki was a standard color for everything from dress shirts and ties to watchbands, buckskin shoes and surcingle belts."

The gate agent announces we are ready to board. A man looks around. A woman comes running. She gets in line behind the man who has been tracking her. He seems to see only her as he asks sharply, "Are you stupid?"

The word "stupid" performs a rhetorical abuse that brings all surrounding eyes to the couple. Between them the word is absorbed without so much as a glance. They're both white and the woman ● is out of a Ralph Lauren ad: dyed blond hair, Gucci loafers, capri pants, a sweater set. The clothes are meant to signal race through class. We have seen versions of this woman many times before even as the "timeless" appears dated. The man is over six feet tall and well groomed in khakis, which were originally associated with middle-class white suburbia of the 1950s. He can be read as middle to upper class, but who knows?

The woman's lack of response to the man's question might be a form of protection for either herself or the man. Maybe she doesn't want to call attention to an unfortunate if ordinary moment between them. Maybe the question seems a minor infraction given what else remains possible. Maybe she agrees with his assessment of her behavior. It's anyone's guess.

Standing behind this couple is another white woman. This woman throws the man a look that earns his attention. Those of us watching see her do it; we see him respond. He says something inaudible to her. She, like the man's partner, doesn't respond.

I'm still questioning what I heard as I settle in my seat. I fell into the moment and turned to the couple only after hearing the man's tone of voice. Weirdly, I'm casting around for words that rhyme with stupid. Cupid. Suited. Polluted. Excluded. Just then

Text *I have watched white people reduce black people not to a single black person but to a single imagined black person . . .*

Notes and Sources In 1996, Hillary Clinton used the phrase "superpredator" in a speech. A year earlier, the academic John J. Dilulio wrote an article ("rant" may be a more accurate phrase) using the term in the *Weekly Standard*, predicting, along with other commenters, a massive increase in juvenile crime (interestingly, Dilulio describes going to the White House and speaking with President Clinton in the essay). He developed the superpredator idea into a theory in the book *Body Count: Moral Poverty—and How to Win America's War against Crime and Drugs*. Soon after these incidents, criminal sentencing laws for juvenile crime became much harsher throughout the country. According to the *New York Times*, the concept of superpredator "energized a movement, as one state after another enacted laws making it possible to try children as young as 13 or 14 as adults. . . . Many hundreds of juveniles were sent to prison for life." For a more recent analysis of this kind of logic see Alex Vitale's *New York Times* article, "The New 'Superpredator' Myth." See also the congressional hearing in the mid-'90s in which Dilulio is testifying on the prison system to, among others, Senator Biden.

Text *All this wouldn't matter if this same category of white people weren't grading tests, funding schools, granting bank loans . . .*

Notes and Sources Most American teachers are white. According to the National Center for Education Statistics' data for 2015–2016, 81 percent of public school teachers and 71 percent of public charter school teachers are white at the primary and secondary levels. At the postsecondary level, the most recent available government data are that 76 percent of full-time faculty whose race is known are white. On funding schools, see the work of Nikole Hannah Jones, including "Segregation Now" for ProPublica, "The Resegregation of Jefferson County" for the *New York Times*, and "The Problem We All Live With" on *This American Life*. On making bank loans: According to 2018 data from the Bureau of Labor Statistics, credit counselors and loan officers are 85.5% white. On hiring, firing, and demoting: A 2006 study by the Institute of Research on Labor and Employment found that having a white manager rather than a black one decreased the chance a black employee would be promoted and increased the chance he or she would be fired: "This study analyzes panel data from a large national retailer with hundreds of stores located throughout the United States. The dataset contains the firm's daily personnel records on more than 1,500 store managers and more than 100,000 employees for a 30-month period from 1996 to 1998." On killing: Recent examples of white people who have killed black people and described their victims in nonhuman terms include Darren Wilson, who said, referring to Michael Brown, "When I grabbed him, the only way I can describe it is I felt like a five-year-old holding onto Hulk Hogan. . . . And then after he did that, he looked up at me and had the most intense aggressive face. The only way I can describe it, it looks like a demon, that's how angry he looked."

the woman with the expressive eyes walks by. I ask her if the man actually said, "Are you stupid?" Oh, yes, he did, she answers before moving on. We are all headed to the Southwest. The Brett Kavanaugh confirmation hearings dominate the national conversation and psyche.

Normally, I would never say a particular white man stands in for white men, because I know better. I have watched white people reduce black people not to a single black person but to a single imagined black person, imagined animal, imagined thing, imagined ignoramus, imagined depravity, imagined criminality, imagined aggressor, superpredator, imagined whore, imagined poverty queen, imagined baby maker, imagined inferior being in need of everything belonging to white people including air and water while stealing everything belonging to white people including air and water and on and on toward an imagined no one. All this wouldn't matter if this same category of white people weren't strategizing tests, writing exams, grading exams, funding schools, granting bank loans, selling property, making laws, suppressing voters, determining sentences, evaluating pain, teaching classes, creating and perpetuating master narratives, hiring, firing, demoting, killing imagined me.

Institutional whiteness has stereotyped blackness and used this particular image to murder by. Given that process, if systemic change is what is wanted, "the master's tools will never dismantle the master's house," as the poet Audre Lorde took the time to tell us. Consequently, I am vigilant that this white man not stand in for white men. I am trying to keep him as someone singular whom I have not encountered in this iteration of my nonspaces in a long while. Were it not for our president, Supreme Court justice Kavanaugh, and the #MeToo movement, I might not, even associatively, be wary of attaching this abusive language to patterns

demonstrated by those representing institutional power; but such is the moment.

Are you stupid? It's not a question I'm used to hearing from grown people directed at other grown people—at least not in the publics I inhabit. All of us, standing around this man, were being asked to hold and normalize the abuse being hurled at this particular white woman by this particular white man. During the four-hour flight, despite my best efforts my mind toggles between Kavanaugh and the man. I think of synonyms for the word stupid, like the word idiot.

The Greek term *idiōtēs* means "private person, layman, ignorant person," from *idios*, meaning "own, private." I'm thinking maybe the couple felt their interaction was private, though they were in public. On some level this seems true for all conversations in public spaces.

Over the intercom system one flight attendant asks if there is a doctor on the flight. Someone is sick in a seat toward the back of the plane. A doctor rushes by with an oxygen mask and a blood pressure strap. Whatever happens happens behind me. I'm watching the flight attendant's face to monitor her concern. She continues offering drinks and joking with the passengers. From her perspective, whatever is happening is not dire. She can hold it without modifying her routine.

When we land in Phoenix, we are asked to stay seated until the passenger who fell ill leaves the plane. The EMTs board and exit almost immediately with the white woman who gave the man the look. She walks through the opened door, but not before pausing to say to me, "This is embarrassing." "Just take care," I say, though I can't help but wonder if she's OK. I want to know what the

white man said to her. Watching her exit, I wonder if her encounter with him is tied to her illness. Something became unbearable. Is coincidence a thing? How did he respond to her? I will never know.

As soon as I deplane, I phone a white female friend who was at the Capitol supporting Christine Blasey Ford, the woman who accused Kavanaugh of abusive behavior, the woman who said in her testimony, "Indelible in the hippocampus is the laughter. The uproarious laughter . . . at my expense." Why does that detail come back to me? I don't know. Something feels lost . . . something with a beating heart.

Text *Not to mention—whose boys get to be boys?*

Notes and Sources The US Government Accountability Office published *Discipline Disparities for Black Students, Boys, and Students with Disabilities* in 2018. According to the GAO's analysis, in the 2013–14 school year, "black students accounted for 15.5 percent of all public school students, but represented about 39 percent of students suspended from school." The Sentencing Project reported that "in 2001, black children were four times more likely to be incarcerated than white children." But in 2015, black children were five times more likely than white children to be incarcerated. According to a report by the National Association of Social Workers, *The Color of Juvenile Transfer*, "Black youth are approximately 14% of the total youth population, but 47.3% of the youth who are transferred to adult court by juvenile court judges who believe the youth cannot benefit from the services of their court. Black youth are 53.1% of youth transferred for person offenses despite the fact that black and white youth make up an equal percentage of youth charged with person offenses, 40.1% and 40.5% respectively, in 2015." A 2014 study by five psychologists, *The Essence of Innocence*: *Consequences of Dehumanizing Black Children*, found "converging evidence that Black boys are seen as older and less innocent and that they prompt a less essential conception of childhood than do their White same-age peers. Further, our findings demonstrate that the Black/ape association predicted actual racial disparities in police violence toward children." Individual high-profile cases of boys being violently accosted or arrested for no cause include:

• Brennan Walker
• Tamir Rice
• Trayvon Martin
• Kalief Browder

My friend answers her cell with the first question: Are you okay? Me, I'm fine, I say before telling her about the couple and the woman on the plane. I ask if women are less tolerant of abusive behavior by men in our current political climate. She says many women at the protest were wearing "WOMEN FOR KAVANAUGH" T-shirts. Sometimes they had signs calling for "Due Process" and "Protect Our Sons." She tells me that in televised interview after interview women and mothers are saying, "Boys will be boys."

How their sons have morphed into Kavanaugh defies a certain logic but, whatever. Don't they have daughters? I ask. Don't they matter? I ask these questions even as I know that what matters is the wealth, power, and access that proximity affords, whether actual or aspirational, in the office or at the altar. Not to mention— whose boys get to be boys? I begin to think isn't this too simple • even as I know on a certain level the apparent simplicity of it is what keeps the power dynamics in place, and whiteness in power.

complicit freedoms

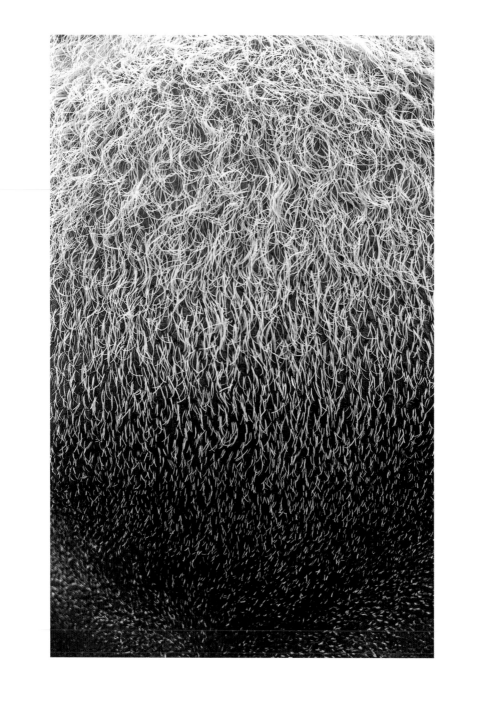

What gave the dinner's formality away was the recognition that when someone spoke on the other end of the long table, everyone listened for the single conversation involving the invited guest. This meant the complete guest list heard when the woman asked me what to tell her black female students who bleach their hair blond.

It was unusual at these academic events to find myself at a table populated by people of color, but here I was at a formal dinner attempting to pass itself off as an intimate supper, surrounded by other black women and a few black men. Sometimes these meals are an opportunity for faculty to visit and catch up about the kids or the terror in their department or the bits and pieces that give nothing away but a random day's activity. But sometimes these meals are a disguised Q&A slotted into the dinner hour.

The professor didn't offer up the name of her course, but I imagined a roomful of black blonds in a class titled the History of Black Power Movements, or Angela Davis to Audre Lorde to Kimberlé

Text *I tried to remember what hooks said, and the phrase "come correct" came to mind, though I don't think it's from that essay.*

Fact Check Yes—the phrase does not appear in "Straightening Our Hair."

Notes and Sources hooks does use the phrase in her book *Rock My Soul: Black People and Self-Esteem*: "Self-responsibility means we are willing to 'come correct' and be accountable for our actions, for what we say and what we do."

Crenshaw: Politics of Resistance, or Becky with the Good Hair: Call-Out Culture in the Twenty-First Century. The one who asked the question was sharply attentive and carried worry on her face as if her students' grooming choices were a reflection of her very being, which is, not coincidentally, tied to her teaching.

The professor's almond-colored eyes were waiting for an answer, and the room waited with her. I could have said we expect too much from one another, but that's not an answer. I could have dodged the question by suggesting that bell hooks pretty much covered this in "Straightening Our Hair." I tried to remember what hooks said, and the phrase "come correct" came to mind, ●
though I don't think it's from that essay.

Instead of answering, I found myself identifying with the scolded and falling into a defensive posture. I asked, in a tone that sounded more like a statement than a question, whether the abandonment of their natural hair color is of equal importance to the safeguarding of their sense of agency and freedom. Whatever the fuck as long as they are coming to class might be heard beneath "Well, can't they own everything in their 'blonded life,'" to quote Frank Ocean. I asked the professor by telling her, and she nodded the way one does when someone brings up First Amendment rights after some white supremacist terrorist wants to demonstrate on the main street of one's town. Some things should matter more, no matter the law, no matter our individual freedoms, no matter— that's what she didn't say aloud, but that is what the nod managed to signify. Her silence made me want to try again, and in any case we were in that room together until someone politely turned our attention toward dessert.

Text *mother-aunt-teacher-Michelle-Obama-moment-of-black-exceptional-straightened-shoulder-length-Madam-C. J. Walker-hair-beauty*

Notes and Sources Carina Spaulding, "From Brandy to Beyoncé: Celebrity and the Black Haircare Industry Since 1992," in *African American Culture and Society after Rodney King: Provocations and Protests, Progression and "Post-Racialism"*: "The growth of websites dedicated to natural hair has led to what is becoming known as the 'natural hair *movement*,' thus rhetorically reflecting the size of its increasing popularity."

Text *We had been told this in all our decades, though no one was talking especially to us, meaning, of course, to black women, since "all the women are white . . ."*

Fact Check Yes, phrase from title below.

Notes and Sources *All the Women Are White, All the Blacks Are Men, But Some of Us Are Brave: Black Women's Studies*, edited by Akasha (Gloria T.) Hull, Patricia Bell Scott, and Barbara Smith.

Perhaps somewhere beneath and despite it all—where the all is every mother-aunt-teacher-Michelle-Obama-moment-of-black-exceptional-straightened-shoulder-length-Madam-C. J. Walker-hair-beauty—was the nagging belief that blonds have more—more of something. We had been told this in all our decades, though no one was talking especially to us, meaning, of course, to black women, since "all the women are white . . . ," though we, black women, are a part of the "we" in the gender conversations the media has with women in television commercials, films, and print ads bombarding us. Blond hair need not mean human, it need not mean feminine, it need not mean Anglo or angel; clearly, it doesn't mean white purity, given that a change in hair color doesn't cause anyone black or Asian or white, for that matter, to pass out of his or her body. Aretha Franklin remains, after all, with any hair color, the Mother of Soul.

All the money, time, and possible damage to one's natural hair ultimately pales in comparison to what it means to take what is available and own it. Complicit freedoms. Is that a thing? Perhaps the students' blondness is their boldness in the face of racist propaganda concerning beauty ideals. Then the black blonds are inside one of those equations where, no matter what you do on either side of the equal sign, every sum will come to one—this one, what I want. Fuck you. Fuck me. Next. Do you, boo! Free to be. Free to take. Free to fake. Frivolous. Fuck brave. Fun. Funny. Good as hell.

Unless, of course, it's a zero-sum game, and whatever the case, the equation equals zero and we remain here in these United States of America, still in line, still complicit, beneath all our choices, inside all our false sovereignty.

Then a question that is also an answer came to me: What would Frantz Fanon say? I asked the professor. She laughed, which pleased

273

Text ... *I badly want us all to have a kind of metaperspective humor around all that goes into our scramble to escape what Fred Moten names "the false fight for our humanity" that has lasted four hundred years and is not the same thing as fighting for our civil rights.*

Notes and Sources An original source on Jamestown—"He brought not any thing but 20 and odd Negroes"—and a *Washington Post* feature. For a critique of 1619 to 1864 as the temporal landscape of North American slavery and alternative conceptualizations, see *Lose Your Mother: A Journey along the Atlantic Slave Route*, by Saidiya Hartman, and *In the Wake*, by Christina Sharpe: "The wake as the conceptual frame of and for living blackness in the diaspora in the still unfolding aftermaths of Atlantic chattel slavery."

me because now she looked like she forgot to carry it all for a few seconds. It might be a failing that I want people to lose their humorlessness, but I badly want us all to have a kind of meta-perspective humor around all that goes into our scramble to es- ●
cape what Fred Moten names "the false fight for our humanity" that has lasted four hundred years and is not the same thing as fighting for our civil rights.

Mine is always the worry that we are already dying—I mean already dead in the social world that persists alongside the lives we live—as we tirelessly engage tall tales in an endless fight for justice. Or, could it be the students have divested from the performance of exceptional blackness, a performance that will never save us from the actions of ordinary whiteness, and decided on reverse appropriation with all its artificiality and performativity.

Text *I mentioned Fanon, whose psychoanalytic writings address internalized antiblack racism, to suggest I understood the professor's worry was that these women were blindly filling up with self-hatred for their own black skin and natural hair.*

Fact Check Yes—quotes from Fanon on beauty, whiteness, and internalized racism below.

Notes and Sources "I am white; in other words, I embody beauty and virtue, which have never been black. I am the color of day." *Black Skin White Masks*, trans. Richard Philcox

"All this whiteness that burns me. I sit down at the fire and became aware of my uniform. I had not seen it. It is indeed ugly. I stop there, for who can tell me what beauty is?" *Black Skin White Masks*, trans. Charles Markmann

"I am a white man. For unconsciously I distrust what is black in me, that is, the whole of my being. I am a Negro—but of course I do not know it, simply because I am one." *Black Skin White Masks*, trans. Charles Markmann

Maybe we are simply in the latest stage of self-judgment, so stuck, judged or judging, which of course is humorless and which also scares me. It scares me more than bottle blonds and what the blondness is meant to signify, if it is meant to signify something beyond knowledge, something about the wilderness of being, and not simply mask self-hatred and low self-esteem. The worry is that this particular hair color promises "the world" to these women, though it cannot give it. Do black blonds believe it allows them to be seen, maybe to be seen for the first time as human, youthful, beautiful, human, and—did I say human?—most tragically in their own eyes?

I mentioned Fanon, whose psychoanalytic writings address internalized antiblack racism, to suggest I understood the professor's worry was that these women were blindly filling up with self-hatred for their own black skin and natural hair. I wanted to show her the image by the visual artist Carrie Mae Weems where Weems looks into the proverbial mirror-mirror-on-the-wall, though she's using a handheld one. The professor could hang the image in her seminar room. The piece is called *I Looked and Looked and Failed to See What So Terrified You*. I didn't ask the professor if she knew the piece, though its title might have answered her question. Or, Weems's question might lead to a discussion in the classroom about the bleaching or not bleaching of one's hair. Ultimately, it all depends on what happened or is happening behind the watchful eyes of the professor and her students as they assimilated and metabolized the repetitions in our culture.

The professor's worry, I'm guessing here, was that the culture damaged her students, despite our—black women in our middle ages—best practices, and efforts with our own natural hair. By extension, we older black women are shattered, since the younger ones are our

daughters, not literally, and for all our Black Is Beautiful rhetoric, deep within our false sense of sovereignty might remain a vision of black feminism limited by white surveillance of black femininity.

The professor nodded again when I said I believed it's important the students do what they want until they understand for themselves what they don't want. I am a mother, but I am also a daughter with memory. Someone on the other side of the table said she wore heels even though they hurt her feet. OK. Some of us didn't, said another woman, and I can't but think there is a backstory there I will never know. Heels versus nose jobs? Different things? Do heels belong to femininity's aspirational life or white acculturation? Are nose jobs a form of assimilation? Skin bleaching is clear in terms of its destination toward whitening one's skin, but is blondness?

Is blondness the heel, the nose job, the skin bleaching, or none of these? This culture made us, and as wrong or as right as we can be, we know someone is always looking. Amen to that, I didn't say, as four men arrived with trays of cake, vanilla ice cream already melting into the dark chocolate. Though life is not always so sweet.

I was still thinking about the professor and her question as I waited for a friend in a gallery. To pass the time, I counted the number of women around me who are bleached blonds: Natural Blond; White Blond; Platinum; Silver Blond; Butter Blond; Creamy Blond; Rooty Blond; Gold Babylights; Milky Blond; Sandy Blond; Icy Ombré; Honey Blond.

When my friend arrived, I told him I'd counted a dozen women who'd colored their hair blond. He remembered his hairdresser once mentioned that many of his female clients went blond for

Text ... *to the "paragon of female beauty"* ...

Notes and Sources On the association between blond hair and beauty see Penny Howell Jolly's chapter "The Ideal Woman" and to a lesser extent "Hair Power" in the book *Hair: Untangling a Social History*. See the first chapter for an account of the blond ideal through European and American history, beginning in the medieval period: "Two ideals concerning women's hair have had remarkable longevity in western society: it should be long and its color should be blonde. . . . Italian Renaissance writers also established the blonde as the perfect female, her fairness expressive of innocence and purity. Of course this was a difficult ideal for predominantly dark-haired Italian women to attain. Even today in our country, with its wide-reaching ethnic mix, no more than 17 percent of women are natural blondes. Following the lead from classical and medieval sources favoring blondeness, the fourteenth-century poet Petrarch expressed the preference for fair hair that prevails through much of modern western tradition. Praising his beloved Laura, he writes of 'Those tresses of gold, which ought to make the sun go filled with envy.'"

Text ... *beblonden was the Old English word for "dyed."*

Fact Check Maybe. Multiple sources say that the etymology of "blond" is uncertain, but a number mention *beblonden* as a possible origin word.

Notes and Sources There are two major sources for Old English lexicography—Bosworth-Toller and the more recently published *Dictionary of Old English* from the University of Toronto.

According to an email exchange with one scholar, "The word 'beblonden' . . . does not seem to occur in our Old English Corpus (which contains more than three million extant Old English words). Based on these observations, it seems that 'beblonden,' even though it is included in the Bosworth-Toller Dictionary, is one of the ghost words with no solid evidence to prove its existence."

Text ... *journalist Christina Cauterucci reported, "Just 2 percent of the world's population and 5 percent of white people in the U.S. have blond hair, but 35 percent of female U.S. senators and 48 percent of female CEOs at S&P 500 companies are blond. Female university presidents are more likely to be blond, too."*

Fact Check Maybe—quote is accurate, but see below.

Notes and Sources Berdahl: "The percent of women senators and CEOs with blonde hair may have changed since we reported those statistics in 2016."

their weddings. After the wedding photos locked them into for-ever blonded beauty, in white, colored blond, to have and behold from that day forward, they returned to their natural color.

Blond hair has been associated with everything from prostitution to the "paragon of female beauty," but from early on it was always rare, so the word blond meant both the natural color and the act of dyeing one's hair. According to the Bosworth-Toller *Anglo-Saxon Dictionary*, *beblonden* was the Old English word for "dyed." Before hair coloring as we know it arrived, horse urine, lemon juice, and the sun were accepted paths toward blond ambition.

Whether blondness equates to whiteness seemed the obvious ques-tion for the professor. But is it to white people? Does dyeing hair blond mean one is reaching for something, someone, some other body in a fantasy of white-pleasing pleasantness? There's a nag-ging jingle in everyone's head insisting blonds have more fun. Maybe Clairol meant funds. The color, according to Clairol, adds energy to your hair (not sure what that means) by softening your facial features and making you look more youthful. Its website states, "You'll have people doing a double-take wondering if it's really you!" They add an exclamation point after "really you" be-cause we know it's not really, really you and the moment will always need the added insistence of the exclamation, which in real life expresses itself economically in touch-ups.

Most definitely, blonds have more blondness, and this must mean something since, as journalist Christina Cauterucci reported, "Just 2 percent of the world's population and 5 percent of white people in the U.S. have blond hair, but 35 percent of female U.S. sena-tors and 48 percent of female CEOs at S&P 500 companies are blond. Female university presidents are more likely to be blond,

too." Cauterucci credits researchers Jennifer Berdahl and Natalya Alonso, who reported at the 2016 Academy of Management's annual meeting that "blond overrepresentation can be explained by race and age biases in leadership pipelines." Journalist Emily Peck reports that "Berdahl and Alonso also found that male CEOs are more likely to be married to blondes: 43 percent of the highest-paid male CEOs have a blonde spouse." Berdahl now walks that statistic back to 40 percent of wives in the photos they could find. Berdahl and Alonso's research led Berdahl to believe that because blond hair is "only natural to Whites and tends to go brown after childhood, we reason that a preference for blond women leaders is both a racist and sexist phenomenon. White(ish) and child(ish) looking women appear to be preferred as leaders, perhaps because they are less threatening to the status quo of power."

Normal people, not in the wealthiest 1 percent, bleach their hair blond as well. Normal people. It's a conscious or unconscious complicity with the idea that white life is a standard for normal life.

Text *Despite the fact that she's a natural brunette, not long after the public consumed her first films, she would come to personify the beauty and the misogynist stereotype of the empty-headed blond.*

Notes and Sources Both of her biographies say she dyed her hair in February 1946. Her first film appearance that I've found was in 1947.

Lois Banner, *Marilyn*: "[Emmeline] Snively and the photographers also wanted Norma Jeane to dye her hair blonde, because they thought it would suit her pale skin better than her natural brown. But she wanted to remain natural, and she worried about the expense of having her hair straightened and dyed. In February 1946, a shampoo company considering her for an ad demanded that she dye her hair blonde and straighten it. When the photographer shooting the ad offered to pay for the process, Norma Jeane acquiesced."

Does this make the reach for blondness a reach for normality while still wishing for the extraordinary—extraordinary fun, extraordinary beauty, extraordinary attractiveness? Princess Diana, James Dean, Beyoncé are all symbols of that extraordinary—everything.

When I enter "blonds" in a search engine, the algorithm presents rows of white women, and at the bottom of the screen there's Marilyn Monroe in all her Hollywood blondness. Despite the fact that she's a natural brunette, not long after the public consumed her first films, she would come to personify the beauty and the misogynist stereotype of the empty-headed blond.

On the street, ahead of me, a woman holds the hand of a child. Neither the mother nor the child is blond, but the doll the child

Text . . . *after World War II, in West Germany, sexy "Bild Lilli" dolls based on a popular cartoon character were sold in barbershops and bars.*

Notes and Sources See the essay by art historian Carol Ockman, "Barbie Meets Bouguereau: Constructing an Ideal Body for the Late Twentieth Century," in *The Barbie Chronicles: A Living Doll Turns Forty*: "On a trip to Germany, Handler supposedly saw a doll called *Bild* Lilli, sold principally in smoke shops as a kind of three-dimensional pinup. Based on a comic strip character that appeared in the German newspaper *Bild Zeitung*, *Bild* Lilli had a ponytail, feet molded into high heels, and clothes for all occasions. The principal narrative of the comic shows Lilli, scantily clad, in situations were she is taking money from a man. Unlike Barbie, *Bild* Lilli was not made for children but for men, who displayed her on the dashboard of their cars and, more bizarre still, gave her to their girl-friends instead of flowers or chocolates. Handler decided to reinvent this pornographic caricature as the all-American girl."

New York Times: "Barbie's inventor, Ruth Handler, a founder of Mattel, based the doll's hourglass figure on Bild Lilli, a German doll that in turn was based on a foul-mouthed, promiscuous newspaper cartoon character."

holds in her hand has long blond hair. In the history of the blond Barbie doll, historians have discovered that after World War II in West Germany, sexy "Bild Lilli" dolls based on a popular cartoon character were sold in barbershops and bars. They are said to have inspired the original Barbie. Mattel bought the rights to the reproduction of Lilli but not the origin narrative from the post-Nazi Germans.

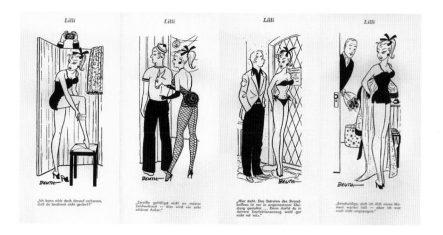

As I look around, I wonder if, for bleached blonds who are white, the added blondness is whitening their whiteness, erasing their ethnicity? In the nineteenth and twentieth centuries, white Anglo-Saxons in the United States persecuted Italians and the Irish, ostensibly for their religion, before they could claim whiteness. Their passports associated them with blackness, and for some, perhaps, their dark hair confirmed their nonwhite status. I suppose if all I had to do was bleach my hair blond to stop white supremacists from wanting to burn crosses in my yard, I might consider blondness myself. Certainly, the forty-fifth president and his family understand the importance of the blond signifier in their campaign to Make America Great Again.

Text *Hillary Clinton, who, like many on Capitol Hill, was once a brunette, also went blond when she entered public life.*

Fact Check No, she was once a brunette but see below—it looks like she had brown hair while first lady of Arkansas.

Notes and Sources See the *Frontline* video from her time as first lady of Arkansas, which describes her dyeing her hair under pressure partway through the Arkansas years (see timestamp 4:00).

I'm reading an article at the doctor's office called "Political Peroxide Blonde Privilege," by the author Amy Larocca. It features rows of photographs of white women in the public eye, in politics and media, all with startlingly similar blond hair. It could be called "Peroxide Nation."

Hillary Clinton, who, like many on Capitol Hill, was once a brunette, also went blond when she entered public life. A *Frontline* program suggests she dyed her hair under pressure. Though she kept the color, she gave up the polish we associate with it and allowed her natural gray hair to grow out and be seen in public after losing the 2016 election.

Did comedian and TV personality Ellen DeGeneres have to be blond if her queerness was to be acceptable to mainstream homophobic America? Coming out was considered a risk, but the concession was the white signifier of blondness. Her wife had to be blond, too. Middle America had to understand that the only difference between their understanding of humanity and this woman dancing her way into their living rooms was her sexuality, which was signaled only by her boyish outfits, not her white and blond body. The title of her comedy special *Relatable* appears to signal the importance of one's likability.

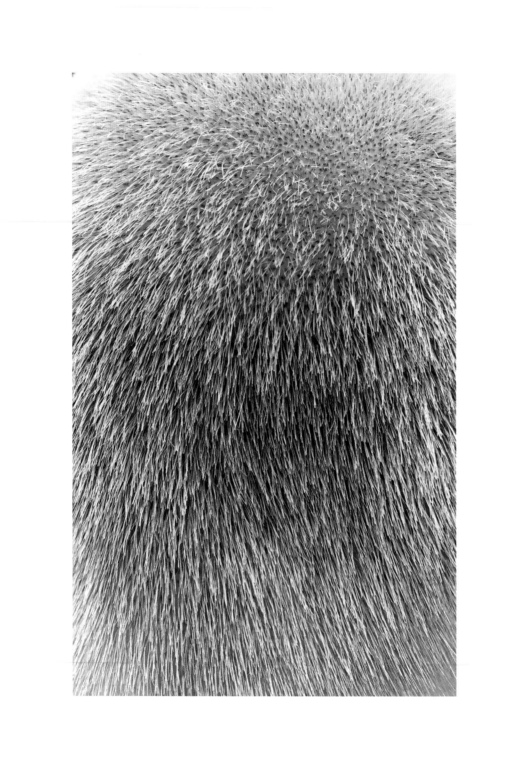

The question for anyone interested in motivations for going blond becomes an inquiry into aspirational living or into the passivity of complicit freedoms. Either blondness grants access to something we feel we don't have, or it feels like a random choice, and the fact that it lines up with what is valued by white supremacy is an unfortunate by-product but not a deal breaker. Another way to think about blondness is that either we are sending ourselves somewhere unattainable, or we can't avoid arriving there in the first place.

I ask a white cashier behind the counter, and she says men treat her better now that she's gone blond. After a pause, in which she might be thinking I will judge her for caring about the male gaze or in which she is just trying to remember her encounters, she says, women also are friendlier.

Is civility what's being chased, the civility that is owed to white purity?

A woman in a New York restaurant says she was blond as a child and pulls up a video of herself on her cell phone. She feels called

out in our present call-out culture and needs to prove authenticity, though my question exists without judgment. At least I think it does. I don't care what she does to her hair. I'm interested only because I want her to enlighten me regarding blondness and the context it evokes. Does it create a sense of belonging, for example? Belonging to what? is the obvious next question. Her blond hair, the woman says wistfully, disappeared with the arrival of puberty. In the video, her siblings are brunettes. Perhaps her youthful blondness meant she was treated as special in her family. But why bleach it now? "Why?" she repeats as if I am incapable of comprehending. "That's an odd question," she adds, without answering me.

I'm waiting to be seated in another restaurant populated by many blonds with only the slightest hint of brunette at the roots, women a friend calls expensive because everything from their fingernails to their musculature to their skin's elasticity has been addressed. I approach a woman awaiting her companion. Why blond hair? I ask her. She's friendly and not afraid of strangers or her truth. Blond hair makes me look brighter and lighter, she says. I like to wear white, she adds. I am surprised by her use of the word "white" as existing alongside blondness. She is the first to bring the word forward without a prompt. Is she saying white only because it rhymes with bright, or does she mean white as a racial distinction that extends from her clothes and hair color toward her skin? The waitress approaches with the woman's companion and effectively ends our conversation.

Not long after, I ask another white woman why she bleaches her hair. She explains more explicitly how it returns her to an idea of youthfulness. Was she also blond as a child? Not really. Hers is

Text *Aryan ideals and their signifiers, such as blondness, were considered superior and were essential to the Nuremberg Race Laws.*

Notes and Sources The Nuremberg Race Laws themselves do not mention phenotype but instead distinguish between those with so-called German or kindred blood and "Jews." However, it is more than fair to say that this was accompanied by a propaganda campaign and on-the-ground practice that elevated "German" features.

For the adoption of the ideal of blondness by Nazi race science, see the chapter "As Blond as Hitler" in Pat Shipman's *The Evolution of Racism*. Shipman also cites a study that disproved the existence of a blond-haired blue-eyed majority in Germany: "Virchow's survey showing that most Germans were not blond-haired and blue-eyed had negligible impact on this widespread conviction."

Potentially also of interest: the "Lebensborn" program in which men and women with "Aryan" qualities would be conscripted to produce more of those features. Mark Landler, "Results of Secret Nazi Breeding Program: Ordinary Folks," the *New York Times*: "To be accepted into the Lebensborn, pregnant women had to have the right racial characteristics—blonde hair and blue eyes—prove that they had no genetic disorders, and be able to prove the identity of the father, who had to meet similar criteria. They had to swear fealty to Nazism, and were indoctrinated with Hitler's ideology while they were in residence."

a nostalgia for a blond childhood that never existed but was presented again and again in the media as a thing cherished. Given that not many people change their eye color from otherwise to blue, I try to think of a single other signifier of whiteness that free-floats like blond hair. Nothing comes to mind, though some people believe indications of a good education or property ownership are readable white signifiers, so perhaps it's that simple: blondness is readable, it points directly to whiteness.

Another day I run into a white woman who tells me she feels bleaching her hair blond is a form of dissent. What are you protesting? I ask. My own normality, she says. She has tattoos that are not acceptable in professional spaces, and her black eyebrows and her blond ombré hairstyle make her seem edgy. Like punk rockers? I ask. Like Blondie? There is a kind of suburban-highlights blondness that she wants no part of in her thirties. I get that. I like her clarity, even as I think dissent is being misused.

The question of boredom for brunettes is frequently offered as a reason to bleach one's hair. To liven yourself up is to go blond. Blond hair as a corrective is now considered ordinary. So many have it, and others, men maybe, aren't bored by it. This raises the question, Are white supremacist ideals ordinary aspirations? I try to consider the statement that blond hair is more attractive and, therefore, to bleach your hair is just good common sense.

Social Darwinists, using false equivalents, steered the world with their adulation of Aryan types. Aryan ideals and their signifiers, such as blondness, were considered superior and were essential to the Nuremberg Race Laws. But are they essential to white, or black, women? Or to the Asian woman passing by me, with hair

IMPORTANT: HAIRCOLOR CAN CAUSE AN ALLER-
GIC REACTION WHICH, IN CERTAIN RARE CASES,
CAN BE SEVERE.

COLOR: **NATURAL BLONDE**

CAUTION: THIS PRODUCT CONTAINS INGREDIENTS
WHICH MAY CAUSE SKIN IRRITATION ON CERTAIN
INDIVIDUALS AND A PRELIMINARY TEST ACCORD-
ING TO ACCOMPANYING DIRECTIONS SHOULD
FIRST BE MADE. THIS PRODUCT MUST NOT BE USED
FOR DYEING THE EYELASHES OR EYEBROWS; TO DO
SO MAY CAUSE BLINDNESS.

INGREDIENTS: AQUA/WATER/EAU • TRIDECETH-2
CARBOXAMIDE MEA • PROPYLENE GLYCOL • HEX-
YLENE GLYCOL • PEG-2 OLEAMINE • POLYGLYCER-
YL-4 OLEYL ETHER • AMMONIUM HYDROXIDE •
OLEYL ALCOHOL • ALCOHOL DENAT. • POLYGLYC-
ERYL-2 OLEYL ETHER • OLEIC ACID • SODIUM DI-
ETHYLAMINOPROPYL COCOASPARTAMIDE • PEN-
TASODIUM PENTETATE • AMMONIUM ACETATE •
PARFUM/FRAGRANCE • SODIUM METABISULFITE •
ERYTHORBIC ACID • RESORCINOL • p-AMINOPHE-
NOL • p-PHENYLENEDIAMINE • ALPHA-ISOMETHYL
IONONE • EUGENOL • m-AMINOPHENOL • LINALO-
OL • CITRONELLOL • HYDROXYPROPYL BIS(N-HY-
DROXYETHYL-P-PHENYLENEDIAMINE) HCL.   F.I.L
#D33266/2. U.S. PATENT: 7,402,108

göt2b Head Turner Temporary Color Spray package warning

as blond as the hair of the white woman crossing the street ahead, both of whom have dark roots the shade of earth?

A friend insists that attaching blondness to whiteness and white supremacy is ridiculous. It just looks better on most women, she claims. I am not white, so I try to inhabit her form of certainty. My friend's unwillingness to interrogate why "better" and "blond" are married interests me. The flip side would be Black Is Beautiful. In Nigerian writer Chimamanda Ngozi Adichie's novel *Americanah*, the protagonist describes how her white employer insists on describing all black women as beautiful. The employer uses "beautiful" to mean black. Perhaps "blond hair is better" and "black is beautiful" are both forms of insistence, with the latter refusing to take hold in the public imagination because of racism, while the former appears to be good sense because of white supremacy. I don't know. I'm simply exploring and not insisting. My friend makes a gesture with her hand indicating we are moving on.

Text *It might be true that many white women ombré their way toward blondness because the world treats them better and pays them more and marries them to richer spouses when they frame their faces with all that yellow.*

Fact Check Yes. Australian researcher David Johnston doesn't mention the timeline that blonds marry on. They do report higher earnings and richer spouses, though. See below.

Notes and Sources From Johnston, "Physical Appearance and Wages: Do Blondes Have More Fun?": "Regression results indicate that blonde women receive a wage premium equivalent in size to the return for an extra year of schooling. A significant blondeness effect is also evident in the marriage market. Blonde women are no more or less likely to be married; but, their spouses' wages are around 6% higher than the wages of other spouses."

It might be true that many white women ombré their way toward blondness because the world treats them better and pays them more and marries them to richer spouses when they frame their faces with all that yellow. They don't even bother coloring their roots or the back of their heads unless they are movie stars or news commentators or politicians or celebrity tennis players and their jobs are to be the objects of the desires of white men, and men of color, and white women, and women of color, and nonbinary people. This is reductive and not.

The "not" refers to the fact that women might be dogged by the sneaking suspicion that they are failing at life without blondness. As a blond I became myself, so many say. Funny. If you say I want to be myself and the culture says the self that matters is blond, then oh, well—too bad—so be it. Shit. After a while, everyone is in agreement about who looks human, youthful, beautiful, human, and—did I say human?

An article in the *New York Times* titled "Why So Many Asian-American Women Are Bleaching Their Hair Blond," by Andrea Cheng, begins with her earliest memory of feeling marginalized by her Asian identity within the white American suburban community where she grew up: "The first time I was aware of my Asianness was when I asked my mother why I wasn't blond. I was 5, and one of only a handful of Asian-Americans living in a predominantly white suburb in Michigan." The desire to belong, to share in the uniformity of blondness, has propelled some Asians in the United States to spend twelve hours and more than four hundred dollars to become blond. Monthly touch-ups to maintain, Cheng adds, "can run upward of $200 a visit." She

Text . . . *Asian American identity is discussed by the professor erin Khuê Ninh. Whatever Ninh may or may not have said about race, the article does not bring up whiteness, though it is implied. The article concludes with a once-blond woman, speculating on Asians' motivation for dyeing their hair, saying that perhaps it was a way to say, "See me." It's difficult not to hear that as a plea.*

Fact Check Maybe. There are two professors mentioned in the article, neither of whom mention whiteness.

Notes and Sources Although erin Khuê Ninh does not explicitly mention whiteness, her statement in the article could imply it: "We're the group that's always told to go back where we came from, and it's partly because we have a very strong immigrant population, so we all get bundled in regardless of whether we're fourth generation or first—to everyone, you look like a foreigner."

writes that Asian women speak about having more confidence by breaking with an older generation and about the merits of experimentation. In the article, the shaping of a new Asian American identity is discussed by the professor erin Khuê Ninh. Whatever Ninh may or may not have said about race, the article does not bring up whiteness, though it is implied. The article concludes with a once-blond woman, speculating on Asians' motivation for dyeing their hair, saying that perhaps it was a way to say, "See me." It's difficult not to hear that as a plea.

In a country that has traded so overtly in white superiority and white purity, perhaps white women are trapped inside the machinery that insists on the authenticity of whiteness. Do they feel trapped? Is the popularity of the ombré hairstyle, blond at the edges, blond only halfway, a way of partially freeing oneself while

still engaging one's entitlement with the vocabulary of whiteness, which doubles as a vocabulary of youthfulness for older women covering their gray?

If dyeing your hair means you become someone else and this person makes you more yourself, is this a sign that whiteness is who you really are? Is whiteness vis-à-vis blondness a thing to own, a possession, property, something that you cannot be without if you wish to live? Is becoming blond a way to access or own whiteness as property? Is blondness an investment that increases one's value by making one simultaneously mainstream and unique in a single process?

The worry is that this particular hair color promises "the world" to these women. Can it be given?

If white supremacy and antiblack racism remain fundamental structural modes of violence by which countries continue to govern, blondness might be one of our most passive and fluid modes of complicity. It points to white power and its values as desirable, whether the thought enters one's head or not. As women say again and again how bleaching their hair lightens up their faces and makes them more embraceable by men and women alike; or talk about their edginess with their new blond cuts; or as nonwhites feel agency in owning a signifier of power they can't otherwise own; or as the gray is held back and valued youthfulness is sought after; or as we reflect back to the world what it values, it becomes more and more difficult to pretend that our freedoms are not bound up with our complicity with the values of white supremacists.

I see a young black woman, college age, on the street near my apartment. Since it was women like her who started this line of inquiry,

I find myself staring. I tell her she looks incredible because she does. She flashes an unedited smile. I ask, I'm just curious, as a black woman why have you bleached your hair? What's difficult to reconcile is the notion that a hair color can be a lifestyle choice, a bit of fun, but can also be in line with a long-standing commitment to white supremacy. Why not, she answers, and it's not a question. I repeat the phrase back to her—Why not?—this time with its question mark, which makes it not a repetition exactly. The young woman has walked on, and I'm left behind pondering—perhaps this is how we free ourselves in order to free ourselves from confronting the history in all time. Why not.

Taxi.

whitening

Are you suffering from low self-esteem
due to the color of your skin?

Does your skin color make you feel
unattractive to the opposite sex
and unable to progress in life?

Are you sick of spending a fortune
on ineffective and often dangerous
skin lightening creams?

Then I advise you to watch the following
shocking video that will explain just how
you can lighten your skin by a whole
5 shades, naturally and from the
comfort of your own home
in just 30 minutes.

This revolutionary skin whitening method
has never been seen before on the internet,
and can be achieved by yourself, at home,
with a handful of ingredients that you
can get at any natural food store.

It's now time to safely whiten your skin
without the need for harsh chemicals and
bleaches that can cause permanent skin
damage, pigmentation and even poisoning.

Now before we get onto how exactly
you are going to whiten your skin,
I want to let you know a little about me
and how I discovered my do-it-yourself
method to the ultimate long-lasting,
naturally whiter skin.

I could picture how much more confident
and attractive I would feel with whiter skin.
I would finally be able to progress in my
personal life and my career with no more
worries about how I looked to others.

Sadly at that point, it was all just a dream.

All the lighter women who were exactly the
same age, and with the same qualifications as
me were managing to get high paid jobs and
attractive partners; and there was me, still
single, still struggling to find work and falling
deeper and deeper into depression.

I knew of these harsh chemicals and bleaches
that many women were using to lighten
their skin, but after seeing so many of them
get sick and permanently damaged from
them I said, "if only there was a safe
and natural way to do this".

Luckily for me, my eagerness to research
into the subject grew uncontrollable.
And it wasn't until after I finally graduated
from medical school when I was studying
cells called melanocytes that I made an
important, and life changing discovery.

You see, skin color is dependent on the
activity of melanocyte cells in the skin.
The more of these cells you have,
the more melanin you produce.
Melanin is the skin pigment
and dictates how dark your skin is.

It was interesting because most people
assume darker skinned people have more
of the melanocyte cells. When it is in fact
both dark and light skinned individuals have
exactly the same amount of these cells.
What makes someone have darker skin
is the actual activity of the cell.

The more active the melanocyte cell,
the more melanin is produced.
Therefore a darker skin color.

It was then abundantly clear I needed to look
for natural ingredients that when combined
would directly affect the activity of the cell.
I knew deep down they existed,
but just needed to find them.

It was an amazing and breath-taking
discovery, and at first I couldn't believe my
eyes! These ingredients that anyone can buy
had directly affected the skin color cells!

Without hesitation while knowing the cream
was natural and safe, I decided to apply it to
myself over the course of 7 days.

My whole life dream had finally been realised.
After just these 7 days I was already
feeling more confident and outgoing.
And this was just the start.

Soon friends and family were asking
why I looked different. People started seeing
me as a more authoritative figure at work.
I even started to get asked out
on dates by the opposite sex!

Everyone wanted what I had.
My unusual all natural cream had been having
a 100% success rate and all my dark-skinned
friends were having great results too.

You don't need to be worried about
washing off your lighter skin either.
As the formula affects directly the cells,
the results are permanent and noticeable
after just a couple of days.

See you on the other side!

A makeup artist and I are shooting the breeze when I ask her what are the needs of her clients based on race? My Russian girls want their lips bigger, she says, making a starburst gesture with her hand in front of her mouth. My Asian girls need to be as light as possible. She adds, I get it. The makeup artist is black and dark skinned like me, so I assume she means she gets how culturally people with lighter skin are preferred no matter their race–colorism.

The resignation in her voice brings to mind an Asian student I once had, who put her head down on my desk when I asked if she wanted to write about her mother. Her mood changed so drastically I feared her mother had passed away and I had inadvertently hurt her.

Without looking at me, she said, my mother is racist. I hopefully responded with my most deadpan voice. Really? How does she communicate her racism? The student, who is a talented writer and a natural-born storyteller, perked up. She said, my mother tells me my father is so handsome, he must have some white in him.

I didn't ask if her mother said the same about her.

There are other things too, she added.

I see, I said. I see.

A 2016 Chinese laundry detergent ad showed a black man being stuffed into a washing machine only to reemerge without his blackness. Antiblack racism is not limited to the United States or Europe or South Africa. The skin-whitening industry across Asia, South America, and Africa thrives in the twenty-first century. Apparently, everyone understands what is valued and rewarded. Whiteness and globalization might just as well be one thing. Or maybe it's just anything but blackness.

I am watching Naomi Osaka, Asian and black tennis phenom, and wondering how she makes sense of the fact that her Japanese mother was estranged from her parents, Naomi's grandparents, because of her love for a Haitian man. The fifteen-year estrangement, which lasted until Naomi was eleven years old, remains mind boggling even as I know this is not unusual.

How does one feel betrayed for a decade and a half because of whom one's child loves? Is it shame of the contagion of foreignness or is it that the purity of one's bloodline is polluted by blackness? Probably both. This could be the stuff of movies; still I can't comprehend how association with blackness, the thought of that, could be worse than the loss of contact with a child one gave birth to, nursed, and cared for all her young life. I think of my own child, whose life and loves inform my life. I try to line up that nonnegotiable love against the knowledge that some lack of association with who I am would be worth the loss of everything, everyone, that one.

Imagine hating a people so much that only when the world embraces your grandchild, only then can you construct an embrace.

Baye McNeil @BayeMcneil · Jan 19
Some thoughts on Nissin's Whitewashing of Naomi Osaka and what it signifies.
japantimes.co.jp/community/2019... #BlackEye

💬 28   ⟲ 164   ♡ 233   ✉

The reality would floor me if it weren't ordinary. The depth of such hatred remains, perhaps, what many refuse to understand.

Osaka beat Serena Williams in the 2018 US Open where all manner of absurdity occurred. In the week following Osaka's Grand Slam win an Australian cartoonist portrayed Williams in what many understood to be a stereotypical racist manner and portrayed Osaka as blond. The whitening of Osaka since her rise has been a dynamic she has been forced to comment on. Advertisements by one of her Japanese sponsors, Nissin Foods, lightened her skin as she was portrayed hitting the ball in her tennis whites. Unfortunate but unintentionally racist was Osaka's take: "I'm tan. It's pretty obvious. . . . But I definitely think the next time they try to portray me or something, I feel like they should talk to me about it." Unlike the Australian cartoonist, Nissin, at least, did not color her hair blond, though Osaka has been known to dye the ends of her hair blond. Why not.

One tweeter noted that at least sponsors are not doing "blacker" portraits of Osaka. The whitening was in some ways, the responder seemed to imply, the lesser of two evils. Perhaps her sponsors by lightening her skin are only trying to protect her and their products from anticipated Japanese antiblack racism. Justified? After Osaka's 2019 win at the Toray Pan Pacific Open in the country of her birth and citizenship the comedy team A Masso at an event stated that Osaka "needed some bleach." According to an article in the *Root* by Maiysha Kai, other hāfu or mixed-raced individuals have been referred to as kurombo, Japan's version of the N-word. As Osaka gets framed as her generation's Serena Williams, we begin to understand her succession as forming inside a similar racist frame.

In press conference after press conference, Osaka responds to the racist rhetoric targeting her, and as I note her wariness, I wonder if she would receive the same treatment if she were Haitian Filipino, Haitian Chinese, Haitian Vietnamese, Haitian Korean, Haitian Indian, etc. What are the Asian countries where the people believe their "origin stories" are not tainted by their association to blackness? I am thinking their anxiety, if anxiety exists, is enmeshed with how blackness is viewed in the white imaginary. And given this possibility, who are the Asians who understand themselves to be so-called "junior partners" within the structures of white supremacy? Obama received 62 and 73 percent of the votes from Asian Americans in the 2008 and 2012 elections. What did they believe our first black president could safeguard for them?

liminal spaces iii

Text *The theorist Barbara Johnson suggested whatever narratives exist are "already read."*

Notes and Sources Barbara Johnson, "The Critical Difference: BartheS/BalZac": "First, it implies that a single reading is composed of the already-read, what we can see in a text the first time is already in us, not in it; in us insofar as we ourselves are a stereotype, an already read text; and in the text only to the extent that the already-read is that aspect of a text that it must have in common with its reader in order for it to be readable at all."

My friend says the gravitational force of an origin story is difficult to get over.

I am thinking of white supremacy.

How many narratives are there for black people in the white imaginary?

The theorist Barbara Johnson suggested whatever narratives exist ● are "already read."

I would add that, in the end, all the narratives end up naming blacks with words that begin with the letter "N." Nurse could be one. Nanny another. No one, could be yet another.

We're not helpless but we are "conditioned to be indifferent," to use Bryan Stevenson's phrase. All these years of white neighbors suspecting, accusing, or killing black people occur inside the law more often than not. Lynching postcards were delivered through the US mail.

"9-1-1, there's a black man across the street opening his front door. Hurry."

Recall mechanisms of my brain bring forward a question and a statement taken from a mural and a billboard.

How long is now?

There are black people in the future.

Text *Ta-Nehisi Coates wants us, at the very least, to talk about what reparations could look like.*

Notes and Sources From Ta-Nehisi Coates's testimony before the House Judiciary Committee, June 19, 2019: "The matter of reparations is one of making amends and direct redress, but it is also a question of citizenship. In H.R. 40, this body has a chance to both make good on its 2009 apology for enslavement, and reject fair-weather patriotism, to say that this nation is both its credits and debits. That if Thomas Jefferson matters, so does Sally Hemings. That if D-Day matters, so does Black Wall Street. That if Valley Forge matters, so does Fort Pillow. Because the question really is not whether we'll be tied to the somethings of our past, but whether we are courageous enough to be tied to the whole of them. Thank you."

Ta-Nehisi Coates, "The Case for Reparations," the *Atlantic*:

"And so we must imagine a new country. Reparations—by which I mean the full acceptance of our collective biography and its consequences—is the price we must pay to see ourselves squarely. The recovering alcoholic may well have to live with his illness for the rest of his life. But at least he is not living a drunken lie. Reparations beckons us to reject the intoxication of hubris and see America as it is—the work of fallible humans.

"Won't reparations divide us? Not any more than we are already divided. The wealth gap merely puts a number on something we feel but cannot say—that American prosperity was ill-gotten and selective in its distribution. What is needed is an airing of family secrets, a settling with old ghosts. What is needed is a healing of the American psyche and the banishment of white guilt. . . . Reparations would mean a revolution of the American consciousness, a reconciling of our self-image as the great democratizer with the facts of our history."

Ta-Nehisi Coates wants us, at the very least, to talk about what reparations could look like. He's in a conversation with historical memory, the archives, "the logic of white supremacy," an American public shaped by that logic, a structural reality shaped by that logic, and Mitch McConnell, or what McConnell, shaped by that logic, stands for: "I don't think reparations for something that happened 150 years ago for which none of us currently living are responsible is a good idea."

McConnell's is a rehearsed and strategic statement. Repetition becomes insistence morphing into an accepted and acceptable position. Help, help.

Coates is modeling a response to this repetition and what he calls "fair-weather patriotism." He's pulling us back from the ordinariness of capitulation to the built-in violence in white supremacy.

Tell me, "I don't have a racist bone in my body."

Tell me, "I don't see color."

Tell me, "I'm not racist, I'm just not used to voting for black people."

Tell me, "I have a black friend."

And then take in the voting patterns in the US:

Those who voted in 2016 to be represented yet again by this form of violence, the 62 percent of white men and 47 percent of white women, a plurality, how am I to understand them?

How should I understand their origin stories?

Text *How am I to interpret their comfort with children sleeping on concrete floors in detention centers dedicated to the suffering unto death of these children?*

Notes and Sources Masha Gessen, "The Unimaginable Reality of American Concentration Camps," the *New Yorker*: "One side always argues that nothing can be as bad as the Holocaust, therefore nothing can be compared to it; the other argues that the cautionary lesson of history can be learned only by acknowledging the similarities between now and then. But the argument is really about how we perceive history, ourselves, and ourselves in history. We learn to think of history as something that has already happened, to other people. Our own moment, filled as it is with minutiae destined to be forgotten, always looks smaller in comparison. . . . Hitler, or Stalin, comes to look like a two-dimensional villain—someone whom contemporaries could not have seen as a human being. The Holocaust, or the Gulag, are such monstrous events that the very idea of rendering them in any sort of gray scale seems monstrous, too. This has the effect of making them, essentially, unimaginable. In crafting the story of something that should never have been allowed to happen, we forge the story of something that couldn't possibly have happened. Or, to use a phrase only slightly out of context, something that can't happen here."

Text *"Like it or not these are not our kids. Show them compassion but it's not like he is doing this to the people of Idaho or Texas. These are people from another country."*

Notes and Sources Brian Kilmeade

Text *uppgivenhetssyndrom*

Notes and Sources Rachel Aviv, "The Trauma of Facing Deportation," the *New Yorker*.

Text *One hesitates to call them living: one hesitates to call their death death, in the face of which they have no fear, as they are too tired to understand.*

Notes and Sources Primo Levi, *Survival in Auschwitz: The Nazi Assault on Humanity*. Translated by Stuart Woolf.

How am I to interpret their comfort with children sleeping on concrete floors in detention centers dedicated to the suffering unto death of these children?

And then take in the accepted norms in the US:

"Like it or not these are not our kids. Show them compassion but it's not like he is doing this to the people of Idaho or Texas. These are people from another country."

How am I to understand the fluidity with which we continue in our days?

How to understand all our looking away?

Teju Cole writes, "There are no refugees, only fellow citizens whose rights we have failed to acknowledge."

How is it these children don't end up in comas like their European counterparts, refugees in countries like Sweden? Those children suffer from "uppgivenhetssyndrom" also known as "resignation syndrome." They give up on life and the state and a nation that rejects them; they give up on a life that feels like "too much."

Primo Levi described this category of people in Nazi concentration camps, those known as Muselmänner: "One hesitates to call them living: one hesitates to call their death death, in the face of which they have no fear, as they are too tired to understand."

This calls me back to ethical loneliness, to the isolation one experiences when one is, according to Jill Stauffer, "abandoned by humanity or by those who have power over one's life possibilities."

US Court of Appeals for the Ninth Circuit

The Guardian

It's within everybody's common understanding that, you know, if you don't

have a toothbrush, if you don't have soap, if you don't have a blanket ...

... it's not safe and sanitary.

A lawyer for Trump says detained migrant children don't need certain sanitary products.

To give up feels like a form of protection from life itself. Hands up, don't shoot.

But giving up is not a thing to want.

But giving up might be what our lives will look like looking back. Not comas nor emaciated near-death Muselmänner but indifference and tolerance for the unspeakable under the category of helplessness.

I imagine helplessness might itself be a thing to be managed, however.

Why aren't all people actively involved in our present American struggle against a nationalist regime?

Have so many become so vulnerable to white dominance that the pathways to imagined change are wiped out of our brains and our default consciousnesses are in their lowest levels of activity, meaning we can no longer envision a new type of future or even really see what's happening in our present?

In the liminal space in the train station in Boston Back Bay a recording reminds me and my fellow travelers, "If you see something, say something."

But then, as if the automated response suddenly understands to whom it speaks, it adds, "Seeing something means seeing an action not a person."

Who knew to add that?

Who dared to utter it?

Because of racism, because of the assumption of a single public, because of white supremacy, because of nationalism, it implies, first monitor yourself.

The next time I was waiting for Amtrak in Back Bay, the second statement in the reminder was gone.

Why was it taken away?

I sometimes joke that my optimism has been stolen by white supremacy.

Don't be burdened by white supremacy, my friend responds.

The "toomuchness" of our present reality sometimes gives rise to humor but could occasion disassociation, detachment from engagement, a refusal to engage in our democratic practices given how structural and invasive white supremacy remains.

A white supremacist orientation is packaged as universal thinking and objective seeing, which insists on the erasure of anyone—my actual presence, my humanity—who disrupts its reflection. Its form of being.

The idea that one can stand apart is a nice fantasy but we can't afford fantasies.

Text . . . *on Zoom social distancing, wherever—one conversation has already occurred between you and me as our encounter newly unfolds.*

Notes and Sources Steve Neavling, "Black People Make Up 12% of Michigan's Population—and At Least 40% of Its Coronavirus Deaths," *Detroit Metro Times,* April 2, 2020: "'There is no question that the COVID-19 outbreak is having a more significant effect on marginalized and poorer communities, particularly communities of color,' Dr. Joneigh Khaldun, Michigan's chief medical executive, tells *Metro Times.* 'While COVID-19 can infect anyone regardless of race or class, African Americans have historically been more likely to have higher rates of chronic medical conditions such as heart disease, diabetes, and cancer in the United States. We know that people with these underlying medical conditions are more likely to become severely ill from COVID-19.'"

Fantasies cost lives.

Universalized whiteness, that racial imaginary, lives in every moment.

We have to be willing to think about this despite spending most of our days not thinking at all.

In most cases we have already decided about everything and everyone, but real thinking, the affect theorist Lauren Berlant writes, "interrupts the flow of consciousness with a new demand for scanning and focus. . . . To be forced into thought is to begin to formulate the event of feeling historical in the present."

She wants us to "jam the machinery that makes the ordinary appear as a flow."

Even as we exist as people in relation—people across the table from each other, people talking in a car, on a plane, by the water fountain, in detention centers, in prisons, at picnics, at work, next door, on trains, in waiting rooms, in classrooms, at bedsides, in taxis, on the subway, at the store, on the street, in the clinic, at the post office, at the DMV, or on Zoom social distancing, wherever—one conversation has already occurred between you and me as our encounter newly unfolds.

Default positions and pathways might already mean that what I imagine doesn't matter given that I am a black woman.

What would white people have to graft onto their fantasies so they can treat as real the possibility of true change? True equality?

Text *In 2008 and 2012, people of color, in the defined categories of blacks, Asians, and Hispanics (leaving out Middle Eastern and Indigenous peoples to the category of Other), managed to elect a black president despite a majority of the white vote going to white candidates.*

Notes and Sources

The 2008 presidential vote by demographic subgroup				
Demographic subgroup	Obama	McCain	Other	% of total vote
Total vote	53	46	1	100
Race				
White	43	55	2	74
Black	95	4	1	13
Asian	62	35	3	2
Hispanic	67	31	2	9
Other	66	31	3	2

2012 Presidential vote by demographic subgroup				
Demographic subgroup	Obama	Romney	Other	% of total vote
Total vote	51	47	2	100
Race/ethnicity				
White	39	59	2	72
Black	93	6	1	13
Asian	73	26	1	3
Hispanic	71	27	2	10
Other	58	38	4	2

In 2008 and 2012, people of color, in the defined categories of blacks, Asians, and Hispanics (leaving out Middle Eastern and Indigenous peoples to the category of Other), managed to elect a black president despite a majority of the white vote going to white candidates.

Once the victory occurred, white people claimed it as a break in their racism despite the fact that a white majority did not vote for a black candidate in either election. But, suddenly, falsely, it was the whites' possession and progression.

What about Obama? I have heard again and again when I pointed to the continuation of our white supremacist reality in this country.

What about him? I've answered back before pulling up the voting percentages I keep on my phone.

Reimagining agency is the conversation I want to have. How do "all of us" believe again in our inalienable rights?

Agency is right there and I am willing it forward.

Anchored in unknowing, I yearn to rise out of the restlessness of my own forms of helplessness inside a structure that constricts possibilities.

Let me ask you or just tell me why or, better yet, how can we?

But who is this "we"?

Is it even possible to form a "we"?

So interesting to see "Progressive" Democrat Congresswomen, who originally came from countries whose governments are a complete and total catastrophe, the worst, most corrupt and inept anywhere in the world (if they even have a functioning government at all), now loudly......

....and viciously telling the people of the United States, the greatest and most powerful Nation on earth, how our government is to be run. Why don't they go back and help fix the totally broken and crime infested places from which they came. Then come back and show us how....

....it is done. These places need your help badly, you can't leave fast enough. I'm sure that Nancy Pelosi would be very happy to quickly work out free travel arrangements!

5:27 AM - 14 Jul 2019

20,909 Retweets 112,398 Likes

💬 19K   ⟲ 21K   ♡ 112K   ✉

Is this even the question?

E pluribus unum might have been the first national mistake.

Is there a "one" that the rest of us should step out of the way of or map ourselves onto?

And once that pledge is made, what are we citizens of?

We the people are citizens of what?

I won't say again the "what" that gives me pause, but I will quote Fred Moten here: "The analysis of our murderer, and of our murder, is so we can see we are not murdered. We survive. And then, as we catch a sudden glimpse of ourselves, we shudder, for we are shattered. Nothing survives. The nothingness we share is all that's real. That's what we come out to show. That showing is, or ought to be, our constant study."

Appropriate that.

Is it possible to live *E pluribus unum*?

As a naturalized citizen, I am as connected to the ones who say "go back to where you came from" or "send her back" as I am to ●
the democratic process that names me an American citizen. And as unknowable as I am to anyone else, I forever remain in relation to everyone else.

I am not a part of the one but I am one.

A friend finished reading the final pages of *Just Us* and said flatly, there's no strategy here. No? I asked. Her impatience had to do with a desire for a certain type of action. How to tell her, response is my strategy. Endless responses and study and adjustments and compromises become a life. What I didn't say to her but what I should have said is that it's the not newness of white supremacy and the not newness of my inquiry that returns me to the page to reengage.

Our silence, our refusal of discomfort, our willful blindness, the shut-down feeling that refuses engagement, the rage that cancels complexity of response are also strategies. So is the need for answers and new strategies. The call for a strategy is a strategy, and I both respect and understand the necessity of that call.

For some of us, and I include myself here, remaining in the quotidian of disturbance is our way of staying honest until another strategy offers a new pathway, an as-yet-unimagined pathway that allows existing structures to stop replicating. Until then, to forfeit the ability to attempt again, to converse again, to speak with, to question, and to listen to, is to be complicit with the violence of an unchanging structure contending with the aliveness and constant movement of all of us.

In this way I remind myself of the faithful who signed up for the long game. The civil rights folks with religious perspective are perhaps the most admirable. People like Ruby Sales, who remains committed to engaging what she names "the culture of whiteness," always have my undying respect. In 1965, when a white man, Jonathan Daniels, knocked her down thus taking a shotgun blast meant for her, fired by another white man, Tom Coleman, she says she stood between the best and the worst our democracy has to offer.

The murkiness as we exist alongside each other calls us forward. I don't want to forget that I am here; at any given moment we are, each of us, next to any other capable of both the best and the worst our democracy has to offer.

There is no beyond of citizenship.

A stranger tells me he thought the goal was understanding himself as different from but then he came to understand his sameness. He came to understand himself to be living also among other humans who are not white, living within a structure set up to disenfranchise those others.

Arthur Jafa said, "As a black person you know whiteness [and] experience it—how do you contain that and white people who you know and love?" I might extend this to all persons who you know and love. Each one. One at a time.

Our lives could enact a love of close readings of who we each are, the love of a newly formed, newly conceived "one" made up of obscure but sensed and unnamed publics in a yet unimagined future.

What I know is that an inchoate desire for a future other than the one that seems to be forming our days brings me to a seat around any table to lean forward, to hear, to respond, to await response from any other.

Tell me something, one thing, the thing, tell me that thing. ●

IMAGE AND TEXT PERMISSION ACKNOWLEDGMENTS

p. 14   From the collection of Hermann Zschiegner.

p. 18   © Claudia Rankine

p. 20   © Reflective Democracy Campaign

p. 22   Reproduced with the permission of Reverend Traci Blackmon.

p. 23   © Claudia Rankine

p. 28   Titus Kaphar. *Error of Repetition {where are you?}*, 2011, oil on canvas. Image courtesy of the artist.

p. 30   Manthia Diawara, "Conversation with Édouard Glissant Aboard the Queen Mary II" from *Edouard Glissant: One World in Relation* (August 2009). Translation by Christopher Winks. Used with permission of the filmmaker and translator.

p. 32   © John Lucas and Claudia Rankine

p. 36   Photo © John Lucas

p. 38   © John Lucas

p. 40   © John Lucas

p. 54   Courtesy of Ruby Sales.

p. 54   Courtesy of Virginia Military Institute Archives.

p. 64   © David Gifford / Science Photo Library

p. 74   © Reginald Seabrooks

p. 80   From the Todd-Bingham Picture Collection and Family Papers, Yale University Manuscripts & Archives Digital Images Database, Yale University, New Haven, Connecticut

p. 86   © Paul Graham

p. 92   © Mark Peterson

p. 98   © Bettmann / Getty Images

pp. 108–117   Graphic design by John Lucas. Scans courtesy of Beinecke Library, Yale University.

p. 122   © Bettman / Getty Images

p. 126   © Mark Peterson

p. 130   © Mark Peterson

ACKNOWLEDGMENTS

"liminal spaces i" first appeared in the *New York Times Magazine*, in print as "Brief Encounters with White Men" and online as "I Wanted to Know What White Men Thought about Their Privilege. So I Asked."

An early version of "complicit freedoms" first appeared on BBC Radio under the title "Claudia Rankine: On Whiteness," produced by Jo Wheeler.

Included images of blondness first appeared in "Stamped," a collaboration with John Lucas at Pioneer Works.

This book would not have been possible without the rigorous and supportive accompaniment of Jeff Shotts, Fiona McCrae, Chantz Erolin, Katie Dublinski, and everyone at Graywolf Press who supported its publication.

I would especially like to thank all those who showed up as readers and shared their time and brilliance in the making of *Just Us*: Nuar Alsadir, Catherine Barnett, Alexandra Bell, Lauren Berlant, Jen Bervin, Sarah Blake, Jericho Brown, Jane Caflisch, P. Carl, Prudence Carter, Jeff Clark, Allison Coudert, Whitney Dow, Teresita Fernández, Adam Fitzgerald, Roxane Gay, Daphne Geismar, Louise Glück, Sana Goldberg, Michael Goodman, Karen Green, Catherine Gund, Claire Gutierrez, Navid Hafez, James Heyman, Christine Hume, Kassidi Jones, Titus Kaphar, Nancy Kuhl, Charlotte LaGarde, Deana Lawson, Walt Lehmann, Casey Llewellyn, Beth Loffreda, Tracy Biga MacLean, Tracey Meares, Leah Mirakhor, Maryam I. Parhizkar, Mark Peterson, Adam Plunkett, Kathryn Potts, Corey Ruzicano, Sarah Schulman, Cera Smith, Kristen Tracy, Jennifer Uleman, Maggie Winslow, and Damon Zappacosta.

To those integral to the intricacies of my everyday, Emily Skillings, Ana Paula Simoes, and Alison Granucci, immeasurable gratitude.

Frances Coady, thank you for being peerless.

Special heartfelt thanks go to my constant collaborators John Lucas and Ula Lucas for their undying support, love, and patience.

Claudia Rankine is a poet, essayist, and playwright. *Just Us* completes her groundbreaking trilogy, following *Don't Let Me Be Lonely* and *Citizen*, which was a *New York Times* best seller and winner of the National Book Critics Circle Award, the Los Angeles Times Book Prize, the Forward Prize, and many other awards. She is the author of *The White Card*, a play; three previous books of poetry, *Nothing in Nature Is Private*, *The End of the Alphabet*, and *Plot*; and coeditor of the anthology *The Racial Imaginary: Writers on Race in the Life of the Mind*. In 2016, Rankine cofounded the Racial Imaginary Institute (TRII), "committed to the activation of interdisciplinary work and a democratized exploration of race in our lives." She is a former MacArthur Fellow and professor at Yale University, and is currently a professor of creative writing at New York University.

claudiarankine.com

The text of *Just Us* is set in Bembo and Avenir Next Condensed. Book design and composition by John Lucas. Manufactured by Versa Press on acid-free paper.